# The E•Z Legal Guide to

# PARTNERSHIPS

E•Z Legal Forms
Deerfield Beach, Florida

Copyright 1997, 1999 E-Z Legal Forms, Inc.
Printed in the United States of America

**E·Z LEGAL FORMS®**

384 South Military Trail Deerfield Beach, FL 33442
Tel. 954-480-8933 Fax 954-480-8906
http://www.e-zlegal.com
All rights reserved.
Distributed by E-Z Legal Forms, Inc.
...when you need it in writing! is a registered trademark of E-Z Legal Forms, Inc.

*... when you need it in writing!*®

3 4 5 6 7 8 9 10    CPC    R 10 9 8 7 6 5 4 3 2        r0699

This book is sold with the understanding that neither the author nor the publisher is engaged in rendering legal advice. If legal advice is required, the services of an attorney should be sought. Publisher and author cannot in any way guarantee that the forms in this book are being used for the purposes intended and, therefore, assume no responsibility for their proper and correct use.

Library of Congress Catalog Card Number:

The E-Z Legal Guide to Partnerships
        p.      cm.

ISBN  1-56382-417-5: $14.95

Title: The E-Z Legal Guide to Partnerships

# Partnerships

# Important Facts

## *Limited warranty and disclaimer* ▬▬▬▬

This self-help legal product is intended to be used by the consumer for his/her own benefit. It may not be reproduced in whole or in part, resold or used for commercial purposes without written permission from the publisher. In addition to copyright violations, the unauthorized reproduction and use of this product to benefit a second party may be considered the unauthorized practice of law.

This product is designed to provide authoritative and accurate information in regard to the subject matter covered. However, the accuracy of the information is not guaranteed, as laws and regulations may change or be subject to differing interpretations. Consequently, you may be responsible for following alternative procedures, or using material or forms different from those supplied with this product. It is strongly advised that you examine the laws of your state before acting upon any of the material contained in this product.

As with any legal matter, common sense should determine whether you need the assistance of an attorney. We urge you to consult with an attorney, qualified estate planner, or tax professional, or to seek any other relevant expert advice whenever substantial sums of money are involved, you doubt the suitability of the product you have purchased, or if there is anything about the product that you do not understand including its adequacy to protect you. Even if you are completely satisfied with this product, we encourage you to have your attorney review it.

It is understood that by using this product, you are acting as your own attorney. Neither the author, publisher, distributor nor retailer are engaged in rendering legal, accounting or other professional services. Accordingly, the publisher, author, distributor and retailer shall have neither liability nor responsibility to any party for any loss or damage caused or alleged to be caused by the use of this product.

## *Money-back guarantee* ▬▬▬▬

E-Z Legal Forms offers you a limited guarantee. If you consider this product to be defective or in any way unsuitable you may return this product to us within 30 days from date of purchase for a full refund of the list or purchase price, whichever is lower. This return must be accompanied by a dated and itemized sales receipt. In no event shall our liability—or the liability of any retailer—exceed the purchase price of the product. Use of this product constitutes acceptance of these terms.

# Copyright Permission Certificate

# Partnerships

# Table of contents

# How to use this E-Z Legal Guide

E-Z Legal Guides can help you achieve an important legal objective conveniently, efficiently and economically. But it is nevertheless important for you to properly use this guide if you are to avoid later difficulties.

### Step-by-step instructions for using this guide:

**1** Carefully read all information, warnings and disclaimers concerning the legal forms in this guide. If after thorough examination you decide that you have circumstances that are not covered by the forms in this guide, or you do not feel confident about preparing your own documents, consult an attorney.

**2** Complete each blank on each legal form. Do not skip over inapplicable blanks or lines intended to be completed. If the blank is inapplicable, mark "N/A" or "None" or use a dash. This shows you have not overlooked the item.

**3** Always use pen or type on legal documents—never use pencil.

**4** Avoid erasures and "cross-outs" on final documents. Use photocopies of each document as worksheets, or as final copies. **All documents submitted to the court must be printed on one side only.**

**5** Correspondence forms may be reproduced on your own letterhead if you prefer.

**6** Whenever legal documents are to be executed by a partnership or corporation, the signatory should designate his or her title.

**7** It is important to remember that on legal contracts or agreements between parties all terms and conditions must be clearly stated. Provisions may not be enforceable unless in writing. All parties to the agreement should receive a copy.

**8** Instructions contained in this guide are for your benefit and protection, so follow them closely.

**9** You will find a glossary of useful terms at the end of this guide. Refer to this glossary if you encounter unfamiliar terms.

**10** Always keep legal documents in a safe place and in a location known to your spouse, family, personal representative or attorney.

# Introduction to the partnership

There is nothing more exciting than the prospect of taking a great idea and turning it into a successful business venture. America was built on this kind of success story, and every day people dream of—and succeed in—making millions of dollars being their own boss.

Of course, in the real world, only a small percentage of entrepreneurs manage to turn their small business into an international mega-giant, but that's not why most people start their own business, anyway. Creating and running your own business—in whatever size you choose—can be a very rewarding experience. You can be your own boss: with the freedom to work any hours you choose, the power to shape the future of your company, and the satisfaction of seeing your hard work produce results.

As the saying goes, two heads are better than one. That's why forming a partnership could be the most important step you take in starting up a business. You not only reap the benefits mentioned above, but you have the security of knowing that you're not alone in these unknown waters of the business world. Your partner (or partners) will have a different perspective that is sure to add dimension to your business, and there will be more hands to share the work. Sure, you also will be sharing the profit, but together you'll be able to bring in a lot more money as well.

There are many things to be careful of when starting a partnership. Most importantly, choose your partner wisely, since he or she will be at least one half of your entire business. Another key factor is the importance of maintaining accurate records and keeping in compliance with federal and state law. Even a very small business needs to do its paperwork and pay its taxes.

So why choose the partnership? As you'll find out in the chapters ahead, the partnership is ideal for a small, fledgling company. Compared to a corporation or limited liability company, starting up a partnership is less time consuming and less expensive. It is also a relatively simple and effective way to take that first step to becoming your own success story.

# Starting your small business

Perhaps you've got a great idea for a new business. Maybe you're tired of working for other people and you want to be your own boss. Or maybe you've always dreamed of opening that sporting goods shop, or selling your arts and crafts, and you now have the money—or just the guts—to finally do it.

Once, you are ready to start the ball rolling, there are so many things to consider! What kind of business, where you should locate, and where you'll get the money from. But even if you already know these answers, you still have one of the most important decisions to make about your new business: what form of business should it be?

By what form of business, we don't mean whether you should open a bakery or a dance studio, but what *legal* form of business to choose. Aside from things like permits and employee contracts, you first need to choose a type of business entity the government will acknowledge (meaning, for the most part, whom the IRS will acknowledge). There are several kinds of businesses, each with its own variations, that you can choose from. Each has distinct advantages and disadvantages over the others, and each one fits a particular set of needs.

## *Choosing the right type of business* ■

Important factors used to determine the type of business entity you wish to use include:

1) liability and personal exposure
2) costs, including filing fees and tax considerations
3) the available methods of raising capital

4) the ability to attract and keep key personnel through fringe benefits or participations such as stock options

5) the time and costs of conversion

Learn about these different forms so you choose the right one for your needs and your new business.

# The sole proprietorship

The sole proprietorship is the simplest form of business organization. It is a business owned by an individual who is solely responsible for all aspects of the business. The owner is personally responsible for all debts of the business, even in excess of the amount invested. The business and its owner are thus considered the same entity. Aside from a local permit or license, and sometimes filing your fictitious business name with the county clerk, there are few legal requirements for starting a business as a sole proprietorship.

Why a sole proprietorship may be right for you:

1) Because legal and filing fees are at a minimum, there are low start-up costs.

2) There is the greatest freedom from regulation and paperwork.

3) The owner is in direct control with no interference from other owners.

4) Taxes may be lower than with other business entities.

Why a sole proprietorship may not be right for you:

1) Unlimited liability—means the proprietor is responsible for the full amount of business debts no matter how incurred and his personal property may be taken to cover debts of the business (this, of course, is a significant disadvantage).

2) Since the sole owner's death or illness would terminate the business, there is an unstable business life.

3) There may be difficulty raising capital or obtaining long-term financing because you cannot readily sell an ownership interest in a sole proprietorship.

**Highlight**

Aside from a local permit or license, and sometimes filing your fictitious business name with the county clerk, there are few legal requirements for starting a business as a sole proprietorship.

## *The corporation*

A corporation is formed and authorized by law to act as a single entity, although it may be owned by one or more persons. It is legally endowed with rights and responsibilities and has a life of its own independent of the owners and operators. It has been defined by the United States Supreme Court as "an artificial being, invisible, intangible and existing only in contemplation of the law." Think of it as a distinct and independent entity separate from its owners.

**Highlight**

The owners are not personally liable for debts and obligations of the corporation. They can personally lose only to the extent of their investment in the corporation.

Why a corporation may be right for you:

1) Personal liability is limited. The owners are not personally liable for debts and obligations of the corporation. They can personally lose only to the extent of their investment in the corporation, with the exception that they may be personally liable for certain types of taxes, such as payroll taxes withheld from the employees' paychecks but not paid to the Internal Revenue Service and state tax authorities. If the business fails or loses a lawsuit, the general creditors cannot attach the owners' personal property. Limited liability is one major reason so many businesses are incorporated.

2) Capital can be raised more easily than under other forms of ownership. This does not mean, however, that a new corporation can easily sell shares of stock. The sale of stock is highly regulated by both federal and state governments, and obtaining bank loans for a fledgling business may be no easier for a new corporation than for a partnership or proprietorship.

3) Ownership in a corporation is more easily transferrable, including transferring shares to family members as well as selling your interest to another person. However, in many small corporations it is advisable to put restrictions on the transfer of shares, especially if the stockholders must be able to work together. This is generally accomplished by stockholder agreements.

4) The corporation has a continuous existence, since it is an independent legal entity.

5) A corporation has a defined, centralized management. Control rests in the board of directors and its powers are exercised through the officers.

6) Many companies offer discounts, in areas such as travel, to corporations.

7) Retirement funds, defined-contribution plans, money-purchase plans, and other profit-sharing, pension and stock option plans may be more easily set up with a corporation.

Why a corporation may not be right for you:

1) Corporations are subject to more governmental regulations than either partnerships or sole proprietorships.

2) Corporations are the most expensive form of business to organize.

3) There is double taxation, since both the corporate entity and the individual owners have to file tax returns. (This may be avoided by forming an S corporation.)

4) Record-keeping requirements are more extensive with a corporation.

5) Operating across state lines can be complicated because corporations need to "qualify to do business" in states where they are not incorporated.

6) Ending the corporate existence, and in many cases even changing the structure of the organization, can be more complicated and costly than for partnerships and proprietorships.

**Highlight**

A corporation has a defined, centralized management. Control rests in the board of directors and its powers are exercised through the officers.

If you decide that the corporation is the correct form of organization for your business, you must go through the legal steps required to create your corporation. These steps vary in complexity from state to state. With careful planning, most people can easily organize their own corporation without a lawyer, thus saving hundreds of dollars in legal fees. The *E-Z Legal Guide to Incorporation* helps take you through the procedures without a lawyer.

### The S corporation

An S corporation is a special type of corporation that, for tax purposes, is treated like a partnership or sole proprietorship. An S corporation has the same structure as a regular or C corporation, yet maintains a pass-through tax status as in a partnership. Once you are incorporated, you must elect to switch to S corporation status and then file your change in status with the state. You may always remove your S corporation status later on.

As you will see below, an S corporation sounds a lot like a limited liability company. However, there are a few differences that are worth noting, primarily that LLCs often require less paperwork, have lower filing costs, and offer greater protection for membership interests.

## *The limited liability company*

A limited liability company is also a business entity created by legislation. It combines the advantages of a corporation with those of a partnership. This type of company is similar to a corporation in that it offers limited personal liability to its owners. It is similar to a partnership in that it offers the same tax advantages to its owners. Therefore, forming a limited liability company provides management with a great deal of organizational flexibility.

Why an LLC may be right for you:

1) Double taxation is avoided. Since it is not a corporation, there is no corporate income tax. Income is only taxed on the personal level, as in a partnership.

2) Personal liability is limited. All the personal assets of the partners are protected from corporate creditors. Managers and officers are also protected if they participate in the operation of the company.

3) There is relatively little paperwork and record keeping beyond a simple operating agreement or statement of the principles of the organization

4) When a membership interest is transferred, only the right to receive distributions or profits is transferred; a voting interest must be agreed upon by the other members.

5) You can form a limited liability company yourself. The forms are available from the Secretary of State of the state in which you want to form the company. You do not need an attorney.

6) You can convert your present business to a limited liability company and begin receiving the benefits immediately

7) It is relatively inexpensive to establish a limited liability company. It usually costs less than $500 to register with the state.

7) Annual registration fees are low, under $250 in most states

Why an LLC may not be right for you:

1) There is a lack of widespread acceptance because this type of

company is relatively new. Limited liability companies only have been recognized by the IRS since 1988.

2) Multi-state businesses may have tax problems if they conduct business in a state that recognizes limited liability companies and in another state that does not yet recognize them, or if the LLC fails to qualify in another state.

3) IRS rules that apply to insolvency may create problems for the owners of the limited liability company

4) limited liability companies do not enjoy the advantages of IRS rulings when there is a sale of worthless stock or stock is sold at a loss

5) the sale of 50% or more of the ownership of the limited liability company in any 12-month period ends any tax advantages the company may have had with the IRS

6) limited liability companies may not engage in tax-free reorganizations.

Once seen as a daring corporate hybrid, the LLC is now praised for its organizational flexibility and innovation. It combines the best feature of corporate protection with the significant tax advantage of a partnership. Currently 49 states and the District of Columbia have regulations for establishing LLCs, however Hawaii does not currently recognize LLCs.

# The partnership

A partnership is a legal entity that is jointly owned by two or more individuals (although in some cases partners may also be corporations or other entities). As with the sole proprietorship, the owners are in direct control of their own company while also personally liable for all debts of the firm. With a limited partnership, there may be partners who have limited liability, however one partner, known as the general partner, still must have unlimited liability.

Why a partnership may be right for you:

1) Moderate filing fees and franchise taxes result in low start-up costs.

2) It has the ability to restrict the liability of limited partners.

3) It has a broader management base than a sole proprietorship, and a more flexible management structure than a corporation.

**Highlights**

As with the sole proprietorship, the owners are in direct control of their own company while also personally liable for all debts of the firm.

4) There are possible tax advantages. A partnership avoids the double taxation of corporations and because income can be taxed at personal income rates. (However, the personal income situations of the partners could also make this a disadvantage.)

5) Additional sources of capital and leverage by adding limited and special partners.

6) The business does not automatically cease to exist upon the death or withdrawal of one partner. The duration of the entity may also be limited to a stated time, or may continue indefinitely by amendment.

7) It is easy to convert upon dissolution to another business entity.

Why a partnership may not be right for you:

1) The personal assets of the general partners are available to satisfy partnership debts, resulting in the unlimited liability of at least one partner (in a limited partnership) and possibly all partners (in a regular partnership).

2) Obtaining large sums of capital can be difficult, as the financing cannot be obtained through a public stock offering.

3) The acts of just one partner, even unauthorized acts, may bind all the partners.

4) Most tax-supported fringe benefits, such as pension and profit-sharing arrangements, are unavailable to partnerships.

CHAPTER

# The general partnership

Aside from the sole proprietorship, the partnership is probably the oldest form of business entity. In the United States, formal legislation regarding partnerships dates back to the Partnership Act of 1890 and is based on even older English law. In 1914, the National Conference of Commissioners of Uniform State Laws approved the Uniform Partnership Act (UPA), and two years later the Uniform Limited Partnership Act (ULPA), and almost every state adopted these guidelines. In recent years, the Revised Uniform Partnership Act (RUPA), which streamlined the original Act of 1914, has been or will soon be adopted by about half of the states.

For a small business, a partnership is usually the ideal structure. As mentioned in Chapter 1, a partnership is simply a legal entity owned by two or more individuals (or corporations or other entities). Depending on which type of partnership you choose, one, some or all of the partners must be personally liable for all debts of the firm. By retaining liability, the IRS allows the company's tax to "pass through" the business; in other words, the company pays no tax, only the partners pay tax on their share of the company's profit or loss, along with their personal income. A corporation, on the other hand, has to pay its taxes directly to the IRS, and each member also pays tax on distributions received.

There are three main types of partnerships, and each one bears consideration. In this chapter, we will give present a brief overview of each type, but all will be discussed in greater length later in this guide.

## General partnership

The general partnership is your typical partnership, with partners who share (for the most part) equal responsibility for contributions as well as sharing in profits. All partners have an equal and active role in the management of the business as well. One should be careful, however, since all partners are liable for any business debt, including the attachment of their personal assets, and the actions of any one partner are binding upon all other partners. This means that, even if the partners disagreed or had no knowledge of one of the partner's actions, they are all still liable for those actions. For this reason, a limited partnership is often recommended instead.

## Limited partnership

Limited partnerships are run like any general partnership, except all partners are not equal. A limited partner is one who contributes assets to the business but has no say in the affairs of the company. In exchange, he or she receives distributions and enjoys limited liability. A limited partner's assets cannot be attached if the company loses money or incurs debt. Limited partners can only lose their original investment. A limited partner is usually an investor who wishes to lend his or her money to a company in exchange for a percentage of profits as the company grows. Once limited partners take an active role in running the business, however, they lose their protection from liability.

The advantage of the limited partnership is that only the general partner is liable for debts incurred by the business. The most popular form of limited partnership—where a general partnership is the general partner and individual limited partners are investors—offers the best protection for all involved. Should something happen, only the general partner is personally liable for any partnership debts.

It has also been popular to create a limited partnership among family members (called a family limited partnership). Technically no different than any other limited partnership, a family can use this entity to take advantage of tax benefits, to protect family wealth, and for estate planning.

## Limited liability partnership

Limited liability partnerships (often called LLPs) are special partnerships restricted to certain types of businesses, such as doctors,

**Highlight**

The advantage of the limited partnership is that only the general partner is liable for debts incurred by the business.

lawyers, architects and other professional occupations. In addition to the reasons for forming a partnership, there are the licenses, insurance and other requirements for that particular profession. Also, states differ in how they treat LLPs. Since there are numerous requirements, restrictions and rules governing LLPs, their scope is too broad to be covered in this guide. If an LLP is the form of business you are considering, you should seek professional assistance.

## *Advantages of a partnership* ■■■■■■

**Highlight**

Aside from lower operating and filing costs, a partnership has quite a few advantages over a corporation, the most significant one being a reduced tax rate.

The complete control of a sole proprietorship may seem appealing, but if something happens (say you are injured or have a family emergency) your business could suffer. With a partnership, you have a partner to share in the work and be there when you need a back-up. And the partners still maintain centralized management of the business. Again, keep in mind that you should be very careful in selecting your partner or partners, as you will have to trust them with your business' life.

Aside from lower operating and filing costs, a partnership has quite a few advantages over a corporation, the most significant one being a reduced tax rate. Corporations as businesses are taxed, thus lowering net profits available, and any individuals receiving distributions from the corporation are also taxed personally on profits they receive. In a partnership, the partners are taxed only on what they receive as their personal distributions. This is an advantage, since personal income rates are usually much lower than the corporate tax rate, and the partnership itself pays no tax.

A limited partnership can add an additional advantage—taking on limited partners can offer much larger investment opportunities without diluting control of the company. In Chapter 6, you will find out more about forming a limited partnership.

CHAPTER

# Getting started

## *Naming your partnership*

Whether your business is a two-person partnership or a multi-million dollar corporation, one of the first (and most important) decisions to be made is what to call your company. Naturally you want to be as creative as possible so that your name will attract customers, but the significance of your company name goes further than that.

### *Names you can and can't have*

The first obstacle, other than your own originality, will be state statutes, which prohibit the use of certain words. If you're a partnership, you also cannot use abbreviations used for corporations or LLCs, such as Inc. or Ltd. Co. Many other words typically cannot be used, since they are used for organizations whose types of business require special licensing or regulation (see Chapter 7).

Not all states have the same prohibitions, so you should check the laws of your particular state. However, words that typically cannot be used include:

| | | | |
|---|---|---|---|
| Bank | Insurance | Lawyer | Thrift |
| Banking | Acceptance | State Police | Lawyer |
| Cooperative | Pharmacy | Engineering | Doctor |
| Credit Union | Underwriter | Guaranty | Endowment |
| Trust | Medical | Loan | Urban Development |
| National | Architect | Mortgage | Urban Relocation |
| Federal | Indemnity | Savings | Certified Accountant |
| United States | | | Chamber of Commerce |

### *Availability*

Once you've decided on a name, you must find out if the name you want is already being used by someone else, whether by a corporation, an LLC, or another partnership. Even similar names can cause problems, because most states will not allow a name that is the same or "deceptively similar" to a name already on record in the state. Therefore, your XYZ Ltd. Co. restaurant may be a problem, for example, if there is already an XYZ Inc. bakery in the state.

One useful thing to keep in mind is to choose a descriptive word along with a proper name for your corporation; perhaps XYZ Foods Ltd, or XYZ Restaurant LLC., in the above example, would be accepted, whereas XYZ Ltd. Co. might be refused on the basis of its being "deceptively similar" to the XYZ, Inc. already in existence.

### *Reserving your name*

Materials you can obtain from the Secretary of State will help you learn how to reserve the name. Usually it is done by submitting a letter or a form with the required fee and waiting to receive clearance. In some cases you can check the availability of the name with a telephone call. Keep in mind that many states charge a separate fee for reserving a company name in addition to a registration filing fee.

If there is any possibility you will do business outside of your state (including through the internet) you will also need to check your name with the U.S. Patent and Trademark Office. Another business already registered with a similar name could legally prevent you from using your name. Even if you were well-known by the name for years in your area, a registered business in another state could force you to change it, and you could lose a lot of business based on customer recognition.

Remember, however, that a similar name could be allowed if the two companies were in two very different lines of business. For example, XYZ, Corp., a restaurant chain, could have a problem if there already exists a well-known XYZ Ltd. that sells baked goods, but XYZ Manufacturers, a textile producer, may be approved. Always check for a name's availability before getting your business started.

### *Fictitious name*

If you are planning to conduct business under a fictitious name, you will need to file for this also. Procedures vary from area to area, and usually your local court or county clerk can give you the information you need. Most often registering a fictitious name involves filing a form called

**Highlight**

Another business already registered with a similar name could legally prevent you from using your name; even if you were well-known by the name for years in your area, you could be forced to change it and lose a lot of business based on customer recognition.

*Conduct of Business Under an Assumed Name* or "dba" for "doing business as" form, for a nominal fee. Some states also require you to publish the name in a local newspaper, so be sure to ask the clerk. A "dba" form is available from E-Z Legal Forms for either individuals, partnerships or corporations, and can be purchased in a pack of ten forms at most office supply stores (and probably where you purchased this guide).

# *Registering your partnership*

**Highlight**

Most often registering a fictitious name involves filing a form called *Conduct of Business Under an Assumed Name* or "dba" for "doing business as" form, for a nominal fee.

The next step in forming your partnership is to decide where to register your company. It would seem obvious to register in the state where you are located, but there may be advantages to registering in another state. There are two things to look at when deciding where to register: financial factors, and whether or not you will do business as a foreign partnership.

## *Financial factors*

Filing fees and annual recording fees vary considerably among the states; though setting up a partnership is considerably less expensive than an LLC or a corporation, this is still a factor to consider. Taxes are also an important consideration, which we will discuss in a moment.

When considering the financial factors involved in registering your partnership, ask yourself the following questions:

- What are the costs of registering in the state where your physical facilities are located?
- If you register in another state, what will it cost to become authorized to do business in the first state?
- What are the fees to check and reserve your company name?
- Will you be charged a one-time state entity tax?
- Will you be charged annual fees? These may include a filing fee for an annual report or an annual franchise tax or registration fee.
- Will you be charged state or local income taxes? If so, how are they determined?

## *The foreign partnership*

Another factor to consider when registering your partnership is where your primary business will take place. You could register in a state with lower fees, but if most of your business is done in a different state you may have problems. If you register in a state other than the one in which you intend to do business, you may be forced to register as a "foreign" partnership under the statutes of your primary business state. This can lead to a significant increase in filing, registration and administration costs.

If your business is, for example, going to be a retail store in Hartford, Connecticut and you register your partnership in New Mexico, you would still have to qualify to "do business" in Connecticut. The advantages of New Mexico registration would have to be very great to overcome the burden for most small businesses of being subject to regulation by two states. If you plan to do business outside your company's state of registration, you may have to qualify as a foreign partnership in every state where you do business. You would then need to consider the registration factors for each of those states, as well as pay all the fees for each.

Make certain that you do register in another state if you will indeed be doing business in that state. If you are doing business in another state but have not qualified by filing the proper papers and paying the fees, the consequences can be serious. In all states, an unqualified foreign partnership is denied access to the courts of the state, which would mean you could not sue someone in that state to enforce a contract or obligation. In addition, many states impose fines when a partnership is discovered doing business without having qualified, and in some cases partners may be subject to these fines. In extreme cases, the partnership may be forced to dissolve.

### "Doing business"

So just what constitutes "doing business" in a state? The statutes of many states define what "doing business" is. While engaging in interstate commerce by itself does not constitute "doing business," if you engage in such interstate commerce and have a registered office, address or agent in a state other than the one in which you registered initially, you need to register in that state as a foreign partnership. Other principal business activities considered "doing business" are:

- soliciting and receiving orders by mail within that state
- soliciting orders within that state through an agent, sales representative or independent contractor
- shipping orders from a warehouse within that state
- paying state taxes
- accepting service of process

**Highlight**

If you plan to do business outside your company's state of registration, you may have to qualify as a foreign partnership in every state where you do business.

Since requirements vary from state to state, you should consult the statutes in any state in which you contemplate one or more of the above activities.

## *The Model Corporation Act*

The Model Corporation Act, drafted by a group of lawyers and law professors, provides a list of activities which, in and of themselves, do not constitute "doing business." Since this act is the basis for corporate laws in many states, and since it can be applied to partnerships, it is a good guide to what you can do without having to qualify as a foreign partnership. The language reads:

Without excluding other activities which may not constitute transacting business in this state, a foreign [partnership] shall not be considered to be transacting business in this state, for the purposes of this Act, by reason of carrying on in this state any one or more of the following activities:

1) maintaining or defending any action or suit or any administrative or arbitration proceeding, or effecting the settlement thereof or the settlement of claims or disputes

2) holding meetings of its directors or shareholders or carrying on other activities concerning its internal affairs

3) maintaining bank accounts

4) maintaining offices or agencies for the transfer, exchange and registration of its securities or appointing and maintaining trustees or depositories with relation to its securities

5) effecting sales through independent contractors

6) soliciting or procuring orders, whether by mail or through employees or agents or otherwise, where such orders require acceptance without this state before becoming binding contracts

7) creating as borrower or lender, or acquiring indebtedness or mortgages or other security interests in real or personal property

8) securing or collecting debts or enforcing any rights in property securing the same

9) transacting any business involved with interstate commerce

10) conducting an isolated transaction that is completed within a period of 30 days which is not in the course of a number of repeated transactions of like nature

In other words, any of these things can be done by a foreign partnership and it will not be viewed as doing business in that state. If you do have to become authorized to do business as a foreign partnership, the procedure is relatively simple. All you need to do is register your partnership (file a Partnership Agreement, and/or a Certificate of Limited Partnership) according to the guidelines set by the state in which you want to qualify and file it with the proper fees.

## *Financing your company*

Before you begin work on your Partnership Agreement, you need to decide how much each partner will contribute to the company, and the amount of ownership in the business each will have. If each partner contributes an equal amount, then naturally each can expect an equal ownership in the business. If one partner contributes more money, you may need to take that into account when setting up the partnership.

There are several options for balancing things out:

- Instead of an equal distribution of profits, you can require that each partner receives profits in proportion to the amount of his or her contribution

- Partners contributing less money can contribute more labor or service to compensate for the difference

- If more money is needed than an equal contribution allows, one partner can offer the extra money as a loan, to be repaid with predetermined interest and within a specific time period

- A partner who cannot contribute the set amount at the outset can set up a monthly payment plan

- A partner can contribute property—real, tangible or intangible— in equal amount to the required contribution (this is best done with the advice of an accountant or tax specialist)

The same provisions can be made in your Partnership Agreement to account for an uneven distribution of profits. As you will see in the next chapter, as long as you include clauses clearly stating your intentions in your Partnership Agreement, you can create as flexible and accommodating a partnership as you wish.

**Highlight**

If each partner contributes an equal amount, then naturally each can expect an equal ownership in the business.

# *Eight steps to your partnership* ▬▬

### *1) Write a Partnership Agreement*

The Partnership Agreement is required in most every state, and even if it isn't, it is a very wise thing to have. Your Partnership Agreement will be your company's single most important document, since it outlines the structure, rules and method of operation for the partnership. This will not only save you headaches down the road, it could be a legal lifesaver. The next chapter will discuss this document at length. If you are forming a limited partnership, you will need a Certificate of Limited Partnership (see Chapter 6 for more information).

### *2) File for federal and state EIN's*

One might argue that registering your business with the IRS is even more important than your Partnership Agreement! You are required to file for an Employer Identification Number (EIN) with the IRS (and with some states as well) in order to run your business. This allows the IRS to tax you properly, keep track of your employees, and more. There's no getting around this requirement, but it is fairly simple to do; all you need for the IRS is Form SS-4 (see the Appendix for how to obtain this form). For specific state requirements, contact the office of your Secretary of State.

### *3) Open bank accounts*

Once the IRS has assigned you an EIN, your partnership should open its own bank account(s). It's important to remember that funds belonging to the partnership must be kept separate from individual partners' funds, as well as funds belonging to other entities. All the bank needs is your EIN and documents from the state showing that your partnership is legally recognized.

At a minimum, the partnership will require a checking account, although you can open any type or number of accounts you wish. In all cases, only the general partner(s) will have the authority to issue checks for the partnership.

### *4) Budget and recordkeeping*

Any smart businessperson will tell you that a budget and up-to-date accounting of your books will help your business flourish. Setting a realistic budget and sticking to it is not only practical, but it is the foundation for a thriving, growing company. You'll find several forms in this guide to help you organize your finances.

**Highlights**

Your Partnership Agreement will be the single most important document for your company, since it outlines the structure and method of operation for the partnership. This will not only save you headaches down the road, it could be a legal lifesaver.

Begin keeping and maintaining your important (and required) records, such as:

- partners' names and addresses
- Partnership Agreement and all amendments
- Certificate of Limited Partnership and all amendments (only for limited partnerships)
- all tax records (local, state & federal) for the past 3 years
- any powers of attorney
- all transactions and financial records

Keeping accurate records ensures compliance with state and federal regulations, thus maintaining your status as a recognized partnership. It also will help safeguard you against any discrepancies you may encounter later, with the IRS, state agencies, employees or customers.

### 5) Notify creditors and customers

If you have previously conducted business as an individual or through another type of entity, you should notify your customers and creditors that you are now operating as a partnership. Direct mail, certified mail, and/or newspaper publication are all effective methods. Also print new letterhead, billing sheets, invoices and other stationary so that those you do business with know who they are dealing with. Always sign correspondence and legal documents in the name of the partnership as executed by its general partner.

### 6) Take out insurance

Don't convince yourself you can't afford insurance, or that you will be fine without it, especially when you are starting up a small business with a lot of your own capital (and hard work). The loss you could incur—simply because you didn't have some insurance—could destroy your business and threaten you with financial ruin. If you have employees, the risk is even greater.

### 7) Obtain permits, licenses, and comply with regulations

There may be specific local and state regulations you need to conform to in order to legally conduct your business. Many businesses, such as brokerage and securities firms, air transportation companies, banks and drug manufacturing companies are regulated by federal agencies.

**Highlight**

Don't convince yourself you can't afford insurance, or that you will be fine without it, especially when you are starting up a small business with a lot of your own capital.

Special permits and licenses are required for these businesses:

| | | |
|---|---|---|
| hospitals | nursing homes | health concerns |
| barbers | restaurants | real estate brokers |
| hairdressers | food services | educational institutions |
| cosmetologists | notaries | pharmacies |
| billiard rooms | peddlers | newsstands |
| private investigators | | employment agencies |

businesses selling or serving alcoholic beverages

### 8) Hire your employees

Not every partnership will be taking on outside employees, or at least not right away. If you do, however, there is a lot of information to be gathered and paperwork to be done. Some of the things you need to learn about are:

- taxes for your business and employees (including local, state, federal, and social security)
- company health insurance
- retirement and other benefit plans
- unemployment insurance and workers' compensation
- hiring practices (avoiding discrimination)
- union involvement
- occupational safety and health regulations
- minimum wage laws and the hiring of minors

The list goes on and on. A helpful resource for any employer is the *E-Z Legal Guide to Employment Law,* available in office supply and book stores nationwide.

## *Other considerations* ▬▬▬▬

Before you begin drafting your Partnership Agreement, you probably know what your business will be manufacturing and/or selling, or the service you'll be providing. You probably have the details about where you'll be located, how you'll decorate your office, and so on. But there are still a few operational details you have to take care of, such as:

**Highlights**

Make sure you comply with all building and zoning requirements, as well as with environmental regulations.

1) obtaining the necessary permits and/or licenses for your type of business, such as
   - operational licenses (e.g., a liquor license)
   - sales tax permits
   - zoning and environmental permits

   Be sure to contact the appropriate federal regulating agency if your business will involve any of the following:
   - alcohol, tobacco or firearms (U.S. Treasury Department, Bureau of Alcohol, Tobacco and Firearms)
   - drugs or food products (Food and Drug Administration)
   - investments (Securities and Exchange Commission)
   - interstate transportation businesses (Interstate Commerce Commission)
   - radio or television transmission (Federal Communications Commission)

2) making sure you comply with all building and zoning requirements, as well as with environmental regulations

3) consulting with an accountant and/or tax advisor (see Chapter 9 regarding tax considerations for partnerships)

## *Where to find help*

The Small Business Administration of the federal government was established by Congress in 1953 to assist small businesses. This agency provides prospective, new and established members of the small business community with financial and management training and counseling. Check your Yellow Pages for the local office nearest you, or visit the SBA Web site at www.sba.gov.

Counseling sponsored by the Service Corps of Retired Executives (SCORE) is extremely helpful, and may offer free on-site counseling services, workshops and seminars. Also contact local trade associations and the local chamber of commerce. They, too, can give you advice and assistance.

**Highlight**

The Small Business Administration of the federal government provides prospective, new and established members of the small business community with financial and management training and counseling. Also contact your local trade associations and the local chamber of commerce. They, too, can give you advice and assistance.

# CHAPTER

# The Partnership Agreement

You might be sitting there thinking, "Why should I write a Partnership Agreement? There are only two of us," or "We're only a very small business," or "We shook hands on it and that should be enough." So here's why a Partnership Agreement is a good idea.

An oral agreement is legally binding, but it is based on two assumptions:

1) both parties make the agreement in good faith (both sides are being honest and intend to uphold the agreement)

2) both parties can actually remember the agreement as set forth (which is difficult if not impossible to ensure!)

Sad but true, even the closest of friendships (or family ties) can be strained and even destroyed when it comes to matters of money and business. You can avoid a lot of potential problems if things are clearly written and and agreed upon at the outset.

Most states have adopted the Uniform Partnership Act (and the Uniform Limited Partnership Act), and in the absence of a written contract, an oral contract will fall under these laws. So, if you do forego the Partnership Agreement, remember that you are still bound by the regulations of these Acts.

There are certain areas in the Uniform Partnership Act, Revised Uniform Partnership Act, and Uniform Limited Partnership Act that you are able to adapt to your needs, though without a written agreement there would be no record of what you wanted to change. It would then be to your advantage to put these changes in writing so that there would be no confusion.

Should any partner act in bad faith, violate the partnership agreement, or commit an act that would have adverse consequences to the partnership, a written Agreement will provide you the basis for legal protection that an oral agreement cannot. Even if you trust your partner completely, it is protection that could save your business should an event like this occur.

If there are legal problems involving your business, or if you are under IRS investigation, having a Partnership Agreement will help. At least you have proof your business is a legitimate entity. This does not mean that an Agreement will be enough to prove that everything is legal or you have complied with all regulations. But being able to produce a signed Agreement carries more weight than just saying "Yes, we run a business together."

The following discussion focuses on the Partnership Agreement for a general partnership.

## Writing your Agreement

Much like Articles of Incorporation, a Partnership Agreement presents the clauses outlining the terms of the partnership.

### Opening Clause

An Agreement will usually begin with a clause stating:

- the date the agreement is made

- the names of the partners and their addresses

- a paragraph stating that the above persons (referred to as Partners) agree to form a partnership (general or limited) under the terms to follow

The articles to follow this opening statement consist of the terms the partnership agrees upon to run its affairs.

Your Opening clause could read:

*"This Partnership Agreement is made effective this 5th day of June, 1998, by John Doe and Joe Smith, hereinafter referred to as the PARTNERS. This PARTNERSHIP, which shall be a general partnership, shall abide by the laws of the State of New York and under the terms as set forth below."*

### Name and Location

This article simply states the full name of the partnership and the

**Highlight**

Should any partner act in bad faith, violate the partnership agreement, or commit an act that would have adverse consequences to the partnership, a written Agreement will provide you the basis for legal protection that an oral agreement cannot.

principal place of business of the partnership (this address cannot be a P.O. Box number and should be located in the state you will do business in).

Your Name and Location clause could read:

*"The name of the PARTNERSHIP shall be: The Style Company.*

*"The principal place of business for the PARTNERSHIP shall be: 777 S.E. Anystreet, YourCity, New York, 02222."*

### *Purpose*

While not a legal requirement for a Partnership Agreement (unlike a corporation's Articles of Incorporation), a partnership does not have to have the purpose of the business set forth in the Agreement. However, it can't hurt, and it can act as a guideline for the direction your company takes. And as your focus turns to the daily running of your business, this stated purpose can serve as a meaningful reminder of why you created the partnership in the first place.

Your Purpose clause could read:

*"The purpose of the PARTNERSHIP is to create an interior decorating consultation service.*

*"The foregoing purpose will be interpreted as an example only and not as a limitation, and nothing therein shall be deemed as prohibiting the PARTNERSHIP from engaging in any lawful act or activity for which a partnership may be organized under the laws of New York."*

Note the second paragraph of this example. Although the Purpose is not a legally binding statement, including this paragraph leaves the door open for anything your company may wish to legally pursue.

### *Life*

This clause states the length of existence of the partnership.

Your Life clause could read:

*"The PARTNERSHIP shall begin on March 5, 1998, and shall be terminated on December 31, 1999. The PARTNERSHIP may continue beyond this date of termination only upon agreement of all PARTNERS. "*

A partnership may also continue indefinitely. If so, it is wise to acknowledge a date by which partners' contributions are returned.

If your state is governed by the Revised Uniform Partnership Act, you should specify the term for which the partnership will run, with the ability to renew the partnership at the end of the specified term. This will prevent automatic dissolution should a partner leave the partnership.

### Accounting/Fiscal Year

It is best to consult a tax specialist or your accountant to choose the method of accounting and fiscal year that will suit the needs of your business best.

Your Accounting/Fiscal Year clause could read:

*"The PARTNERSHIP shall use the accrual method of accounting.*

*The fiscal year of the PARTNERSHIP shall be from January 1st to December 31st."*

### Contributions/Ownership

This clause will list the amounts of contributions, cash or otherwise, of each of the partners. You should also list here other provisions for uneven contributions, credits to and loans from partner contributions, and percentage of ownership.

Your Contributions clause(s) could read:

*"Each partner shall contribute $10,000 to be paid to the PARTNERSHIP by April 30, 1998.*

*"Each partner shall own 50% of the PARTNERSHIP."*

or

*"John Doe's contribution shall be $10,000*

*Joe Smith's contribution shall be $6,000*

*Said contributions shall be paid to the PARTNERSHIP by April 30, 1998."*

*Joe Smith shall work 10 hours per week in addition to hours as set forth below, for an equivalent of $100 per week, until $4,000 balance of the difference of the PARTNERS' initial contributions to the PARTNERSHIP shall be paid.*

*"Each partner shall own 50% of the PARTNERSHIP."*

### Profit and Loss

Nothing will be more important to your business than the income it receives (or doesn't), and this clause will be one of the most important in your Agreement. The main function of this clause is to state how much of the profits each partner will receive and likewise with a loss, how much of

**Highlight**

It is best to consult a tax specialist or your accountant to choose the method of accounting and fiscal year that will suit the needs of your business best.

a loss each partner can claim to the IRS. You may also include provisions for retaining profits in the business or provisions regarding a draw (advance) on profits.

Your Profit and Loss clause could read:

*"The PARTNERSHIP's net profits shall be distributed, and net losses charged, for each year to the PARTNERS as follows:*

*John Doe shall be allocated/charged 50% of said profits/losses.*

*Joe Smith shall be allocated/charged 50% of said profits/losses."*

### *Powers and Authorities (Management)*

This will be the most extensive section in your Agreement, as it should spell out the details of how you want to run your partnership. It can include clauses covering:

- decision making; generally, each partner has an equal vote and all major decisions must be unanimous, though you may state otherwise. If an individual partner can act alone, you may set limits on the kinds of decisions made alone, since any decision of one partner will be binding upon all the partners
- the type of labor/skills/participation and the hours worked of each partner in running the business
- specifications on how the books are to be kept, and when accounting should be done
- the types of competing or closely related businesses a partner may pursue
- ownership rights to the partnership name, trade secrets, products, trademarks or other licenses the partnership may acquire

The number of management specifications you may include are endless, and you should look to the needs and operation of your business to tell you which clauses are important to include. In other words, if you feel the need to specify who opens the shop doors each morning, then do so.

Your Powers and Authorities clauses could read:

*"A) All PARTNERS shall have an equal vote in all matters, and all matters involving, or having implications to involve, the amount of $500 or more shall require the unanimous decision of the PARTNERS.*

**Highlight**

The main function of the "profit and loss" clause is to state how much of the profits each partner will receive and likewise, with a loss, how much of a loss each partner can claim to the IRS.

*"B) Each PARTNER shall contribute 20 hours per week of labor to partnership business.*

*"C) Within one month of the close of each fiscal year, the accounts shall be taken to a certified public accountant for reconciliation and preparation for IRS tax filings.*

*"D) No PARTNER shall be allowed to participate in any competing or closely related business without unanimous consent of the remaining PARTNER(S).*

*"E) The PARTNERSHIP name, and all trade secrets, trademarks and resources shall remain the property of the PARTNERSHIP. Should a PARTNER leave or be expelled, said property shall remain the property of the PARTNERSHIP, unless decided otherwise by unanimous consent of all remaining PARTNERS."*

### Continuity

According the the Uniform Partnership Act, if a partner quits, retires, sells their interest in the partnership or dies, the partnership is immediately dissolved. You must also be prepared for unpredictable life-changing events such as death or personal financial crisis. Most often, when a partner's departure triggers dissolution, the remaining partners would like to keep the business running as is, unless the business simply can't go on without that partner. A simple clause in your Partnership Agreement stating that, in the event of a partner's departure, retirement, sale of interest or death, the partnership will not dissolve providing certain steps are taken, will be sufficient to protect the business no matter what happens to any partner.

Your Continuity clause could read:

*"Upon the retirement, withdrawal, expulsion, inability to function as a partner due to disability or otherwise, or upon the death of any partner, the PARTNERSHIP shall not dissolve or terminate, but shall continue its business without interruption under the terms set forth in this Partnership Agreement."*

### Departures

Under the UPA, the departure of a partner will result in the immediate dissolution of the partnership, unless specific procedures for a departure are set forth in an Agreement. (Under the RUPA, this is not the case as long as you have stated the specified purpose and/or agreed term for which the partnership is formed.) This generally happens in two circumstances: 1) a partner wishes to depart, is expelled, wishes to retire or dies, or 2) a partner

**Highlight**

According the the Uniform Partnership Act, if a partner quits, retires, sells their interest in the partnership or dies, the partnership is immediately dissolved.

receives an offer to sell his or her interest in the partnership. If either happens, you should specify how your partnership will deal with it.

Most often the remaining partner(s) is given the first opportunity to "buy out" the departing partner's interest; in the case of death, the partner's estate must offer the interest to the remaining partner(s). When an outsider offers to purchase a partner's interest, and that partner accepts, a remaining partner is usually given "first right of refusal," meaning the remaining partner may purchase the interest at the price offered by the outside party. If the remaining partner decides to purchase the interest, the departing partner is bound to sell it to the remaining partner.

Depending on the net worth of the partnership, one partner's interest could amount to a considerable sum, and the remaining partner may not be able to afford the buy out. That is why many partnerships purchase "buy out insurance" for just that situation. This ensures that the originating partners will retain control, even if one of the partners leaves.

Your Departures section could read:

*"Upon the retirement, withdrawal, expulsion, inability to function as a partner due to disability or otherwise, or upon the death of any partner, that partner (or that partner's estate, in the case of death) shall be obligated to sell his or her interest in the partnership to the remaining partner(s) under the terms set forth below. Should there be no remaining partner wishing to buy this interest, the sale of said interest shall be conducted according to the terms set forth below.*

*Should a partner wish to sell their interest, and receive an offer to buy said interest from outside the partnership, the remaining partner(s) shall have right of first refusal to buy said interest at the price offered by the outside party. Should there be no remaining PARTNER wishing to buy this interest, the sale of said interest shall be conducted according to the terms set forth below.*

*Should the remaining partners be unable to agree who shall purchase said interest, the right shall be determined by silent bids, and partner offering the highest bid shall purchase said interest according to the terms set forth below.*

*The value of said interest shall be determined according to a method to be agreed upon by all remaining PARTNERS. Method of payment shall be in cash in the amount of 10% of the value per month until paid in full.*

**Highlights**

When an outsider offers to purchase a partner's interest, and that partner accepts, a remaining partner is usually given "first right of refusal," meaning the remaining partner may themselves purchase the interest at the price offered.

*Whenever the partnership is obligated or chooses to purchase a PARTNER's interest, in the partnership, it shall pay for that interest by promissory note of the partnership. Any promissory note shall be dated as of the effective date of the purchase, shall mature in not more than 5 years, shall be payable in equal installments that come due monthly, and shall bear interest at the rate of 5% per annum. The first payment shall be made 30 days after the date of the promissory note.*

*With the exception of death, a departing PARTNER shall not have legal right to the use of the PARTNERSHIP name, names of any*

*products or rights to any trademarks, copyrights or patents owned by the PARTNERSHIP, unless agreed upon by all remaining PARTNERS.*

*Unless physically impossible, a partner wishing to leave the partnership, or sell their interest thereof, must give two weeks notice, in writing, of this intent. Failure to do so will result in the immediate forfeiture of the partnership interest. If no remaining PARTNER wishes to purchase said interest, the sale of said interest shall be conducted according to the terms above."*

Note that, in this example, no specifications were given for determining the value of the partnership assets. Under the RUPA, a partner's interest is determined by the partnership's liquidation value or its going concern value, whichever is greater. However, under the UPA there is no such method established, so you must choose a method of your own. There are several methods you may use to determine your business' value:

- a book value method
- a set-dollar method
- an asset-valuation method
- a capitalization of earnings method

There are also several ways to pay for a partner's interest, such as acquiring "buy out" insurance or taking out a bank loan or promissory note. Despite our simple examples, we recommend you choose a method for valuation and payment when drafting your Agreement. The advice of an accountant, an attorney or both will save you headaches later on.

### Disputes

As with any relationship, conflicts may arise in a partnership. In the running of a business, however, a major conflict could cause great damage. Even partners with the closest of relationships may find it difficult to reach

**Highlight**

Under the RUPA, a partner's interest is determined by the partnership's liquidation value or its going concern value, whichever is greater. However, under the UPA there is no such method established, so you must choose a method of your own.

a solution. For the sake of the business—and possibly a friendship—it might become necessary to find a solution outside the partnership. The methods available are mediation, arbitration, and litigation.

1) **Mediation.** In mediation, an outside party is brought in to help resolve the conflict. The mediator is simply a "referee" for the parties at odds and may not decide in favor of either party, nor enforce any of its suggestions. Any decision reached in mediation is not legally binding.

**Highlights**

In mediation, an outside party is brought in to help resolve the conflict. The mediator is simply a "referee" for the parties at odds and may not decide in favor of either party, nor enforce any of its suggestions.

The mediator helps the partners negotiate an agreement that will be most beneficial to the partnership and acceptable to all involved. In writing your mediation clause, all that is needed is a basic outline for approaching the dispute. State when and where the mediation will take place, who will do the mediation, and that decisions will be put in writing and be binding upon all partners. Note that any mediation without a prior written and signed agreement that it shall be so by all partners will not be binding.

Your Mediation clause could read:

*"Any dispute between PARTNERS that cannot be solved informally amongst themselves shall first be subject to mediation. The PARTNERS agree to comply with all procedures to implement this mediation.*

*Mediation shall take place within 10 days of a written request by any PARTNER for mediation, submitted to the partnership. Mediation shall be conducted by the PARTNERSHIP's retained attorney, at a time and place to be determined by the attorney. The cost of mediation shall be shared equally among all PARTNERS.*

*Once agreement has been reached, the decision shall be set in writing and signed by all partners, and all PARTNERS agree to be bound by this decision. Should an agreement fail to be reached, by mutual decision of the PARTNERS or at the written request of any PARTNER, the conflict may proceed into arbitration as per this Agreement."*

2) **Arbitration.** Arbitration is similar to having a judge decide your case in court, without the hassle of litigation. Arbitration, like mediation, is less formal than a court procedure, and the partners must agree to be bound by the decision.

In arbitration, each side presents its case to an arbiter, who then makes a decision on the matter. The partners then put this decision in writing, sign it, and become bound by it; even a court of law will uphold a decision of an arbiter. Your arbitration clause will seem quite similar to your mediation clause, with a few exceptions.

Your Arbitration clause could read:

*"Any dispute between PARTNERS that cannot be solved through mediation shall be subject to arbitration. The PARTNERS agree to comply with all procedures to implement this arbitration.*

*"Arbitration shall take place within 10 days of any failed attempt at mediation, or at the written request for arbitration by any PARTNER, submitted to the partnership. Arbitration shall be conducted by a party to be chosen by the PARTNERSHIP's retained accountant, at a time and place to be determined by the attorney.*

*"The arbiter shall allow for evidence on all sides, including written statements and other evidence or witnesses. No PARTNER may be represented by an attorney or any third party. The cost of arbitration shall be shared equally among all PARTNERS.*

*"Once the arbiter has reached a decision, the decision shall be set in writing, signed by all partners and filed with the clerk of court. All PARTNERS agree to be bound by this decision."*

### Litigation

Most conflicts can be resolved personally, and those that can't usually can be resolved by mediation. If arbitration is necessary, it is enforceable in a court of law. However, if a dispute or action has caused such severe damage that the partnership cannot continue in its normal manner, a partner or partners may resort to court action. Realize that, by bringing a lawsuit, you will likely incur great expense and emotional upheaval, and that even if a solution is found, the process will probably scar your business in some way. Provisions for mediation and arbitration will, hopefully, prevent this from happening.

### Expulsions

A breakdown of trust is not a pleasant thing to imagine, but suppose one of your partners stole from the business, or you discovered your partner was involved in activities that directly hurt your business. If the cause is serious enough, expulsion of that partner could be the best option. Therefore, provisions for expelling a partner must be included in your Partnership Agreement.

The UPA, RUPA and ULPA have specific guidelines for expelling partners, and expulsions, properly documented also can be court-ordered. You can specify certain activities as grounds for expulsion, but check with an attorney to be sure they are strong enough to hold up in court.

**Highlight**

In arbitration, each side presents its case to an arbiter, who then makes a decision on the matter. The partners then put this decision in writing, sign it, and become bound by it; even a court of law will uphold a decision of an arbiter.

Possible grounds for expulsion can be:

- A partner files personal bankruptcy. Under the UPA, this action triggers dissolution of the partnership, unless you include a provision to instead require expulsion of the bankrupt partner.

- A partner is declared mentally or physically incapable of continuing actively in the partnership.

- A partner is involved in activities or other business in direct conflict of interest with the partnership.

- A partner is stealing from the partnership.

- A partner has knowingly breached the Partnership Agreement.

- A partner's conduct is deemed detrimental to the affairs of the partnership.

- A partner can no longer comply with the Partnership Agreement or contribute needed capital or service.

- A partner has misused or mishandled partnership funds and property.

Keep in mind that, to effect the expulsion, you may need to bring a lawsuit against the offending partner. Always attempt mediation and arbitration before resorting to legal action.

### Dissolution

There are several reasons why a partnership dissolves:

- A date or completion of task is reached, as set forth in the Partnership Agreement.

- There is a loss or gain of a partner(s)

- A partner files bankruptcy

- It is unlawful to continue business or continue as a partnership

- A partner is declared by a court to be of unsound mind or is in any other way unable to perform as a partner

- A partner commits an act that is detrimental to the operation of the partnership or is a breach of contract (breach of the Agreement)

---

**Highlights**

The UPA, RUPA and ULPA have specific guidelines for expelling partners, and expulsions, properly documented also can be court-ordered. You can specify certain activities as grounds for expulsion, but check with an attorney to be sure they are strong enough to hold up in court.

- the court declares that the business can only operate at a loss or that other circumstances make dissolution necessary

Under the UPA, a partnership must dissolve with the departure (or gain) of a partner. That doesn't mean, however, that you have to close up shop the minute a partner leaves or dies. With the Continuity clause discussed earlier, you can provide that your partnership continues business as usual. However, you will need to document the change of partners in writing, and make certain that the share of the departed partner is paid for (as per your buy out/transfer clauses).

On the other hand, you may want to completely dissolve the partnership. Maybe the business is failing, or the partners just don't want to continue the partnership anymore, or one partner commits an act or crime that forces you out of business. Even if you never expect to fold your business, it's in your best interest and protection to have provisions in your Agreement clearly defining the winding down process, including the transfer of assets, requirements for admitting a new partner, guidelines for a partner retiring, and so on. This clause should include specifications on voting for dissolution, distribution of assets, and the use of the partnership name and/or property. See Chapter 10, "Dissolving your partnership," for important points to include in your Dissolution clause.

### Amending the Agreement

Most likely, down the road, you will find there are parts of your Agreement that aren't appropriate to your circumstances. Perhaps you will create a new product whose rights will go to a specific partner upon dissolution, or you want to alter the procedure for taking a leave of absence. Adding, deleting or re-writing certain clauses will help your Agreement more appropriately conform to the current needs of your business. Most provisions for amendments are very simple, though, and only need to specify how an amendment to the Agreement is accepted.

Your Amendments clause could read:

*"All amendments to this Agreement must be submitted in writing by any PARTNER, and must be accepted with the unanimous consent of all PARTNERS."*

### General clauses

There are many other issues your Agreement can address, which have no specific category but are general provisions for running your partnership. Consider additional clauses stating:

**Highlight**

Most likely, down the road, you will find that there are parts of your Agreement that aren't appropriate to your circumstances. Adding, deleting or re-writing certain clauses will help your Agreement more accurately conform to the needs of your business.

- if any part of the Agreement is declared invalid, it will not affect the enforceability of any other part of the Agreement

- the partnership will be bound by the laws of the particular state

- any additions, amendments or attachments (in writing) to the Agreement will be considered to be part of the Agreement

- all monetary assets shall be maintained in a bank account (or whatever form or institution desired) as agreed by all the partners

- the Agreement will be binding on any successors or heirs of any partners (unless otherwise specified in the Agreement)

There are many other issues you may address: what kind of insurance to carry, how to restrict similar business activity of partners outside the partnership, or how distribution of profits will be executed. Talking this over with all partners will help clarify the needs you want to address in your Agreement. And remember that, even if you forget something important, you can always add it later as an amendment.

## *The final touch*

Perhaps the most important part of the Agreement is this last section: your signatures! You can say all you want in your Agreement, but without the date and the partners' signatures, duly notarized, it's just a piece of paper.

NOTE: As we mentioned earlier, this discussion on the Partnership Agreement only completely applies to a general partnership. Limited partnerships are governed by the ULPA and, as you will see in Chapter 6, require a slightly modified Partnership Agreement.

**Highlights**

Talking with all partners will help clarify the needs you want to address in your Agreement. And remember that, even if you forget something important, you can always add it later as an amendment.

# Transferring assets to the partnership

Contributions in return for a partnership interest do not necessarily have to be cash contributions; in fact, very often they're not. You also can contribute real estate, equipment, and even intangible property such as a copyright or trademark. What you contribute to a partnership is called an asset.

## *Assets a partnership should not own*

The assets to be owned by the partnership are best decided upon with your attorney and tax advisor. You must be careful to only transfer assets that have a business, or investment, purpose.

Certain assets should not be titled to your partnership. They include:

1) **Your home.** It is not wise to title the home to the partnership for several reasons. If asset protection is the goal, comparable protection may be obtained through your state's homestead laws, titling the home through a spousal tenancy-by-the-entirety or by encumbering the home. A more compelling reason not to title the home to the partnership involves the income tax deduction for home mortgage interest. Section 163 of the IRS code allows an interest deduction only for a "qualified residence," which is defined as the taxpayer's principal residence. Therefore, the taxpayer, rather than the partnership often winds up paying the interest. It may also be necessary to personally pay real estate taxes to in order to claim those taxes as a deduction. More significantly, a home titled to a partnership loses the capital gains carry forward available to those under age 55 who sell their home and acquire another home of equal or greater value. You also lose the present $125,000

capital gains exclusion when your home is not individually owned.

2) **S Corporation shares.** S Corporations cannot be owned by a partnership under IRS rules. C Corporation shares can be owned by a partnership, as can interests in an LLC.

3) **Pensions and Retirement Accounts.** Pensions, retirement accounts, IRAs, SEP-IRAs and other qualified or tax-deferred plans must remain in segregated accounts and cannot be titled with a partnership.

4) **Annuities.** Annuities can be titled with a partnership; however, you may lose the tax deferral benefits. This would greatly reduce the benefits of purchasing an annuity. Never title annuities or any other asset to your partnership unless first approved by your tax advisor.

## Assets a partnership can own

One advantage of the partnership is that it can protect a wide number of personal or business-related assets. The following assets can legally be owned by the partnership, and titling these assets with the partnership should be considered as part of the funding process:

| | |
|---|---|
| Vacation home | Rental/commercial property |
| Time-share units | Automobiles |
| Vacant land | Boats |
| Farm land | Airplanes |
| Life insurance | Money market funds |
| Mutual funds | Stocks and bonds |
| Business inventory | Business equipment and supplies |
| Patents | Accounts receivable |
| Trademarks | Jewelry |
| Copyrights | Antiques and art |
| Other proprietary rights | Mortgages/notes receivable |
| Contract rights | Judgments and claims against others |
| C corporation shares in closely-held corporations | |

**Highlight**

S Corporation cannot be owned by a partnership under IRS rules. C Corporation shares can be owned by a partnership as can interests in an LLC.

## *Selecting assets*

There is a difference between assets your partnership *can* own and assets it *should* own. The partnership may not be the ideal entity in which to title certain assets, although it would be legally permissible. Consider these points when selecting assets for your partnership to own:

- **Purpose of the partnership**: If the partnership is to have a specific business purpose, then the partnership should contain only those assets necessary to fulfill that function. For example, a partnership organized to develop real estate should not logically contain extraneous and unrelated assets, such as personal investments, e.g. mutual funds.

- **The transfer expense**: It may not always be justified to transfer certain assets. For example, if you plan to sell investment properties, is it worthwhile to paying legal and transfer costs associated with temporary retitling to the partnership?

- **Taxes**: What consequences would a transfer have on your estate plan or tax picture?

- **Ease of transference**: How easily can you transfer the asset? Is it jointly owned, or would a transfer disrupt present arrangements, relationships or organizational structures?

- **Ownership**: Will you own the partnership with other partners and prefer to retain sale control and ownership of the asset?

## *Transferring assets to the partnership*

The procedures used to transfer assets to the partnership are the same as those used for transferring assets to any other entity or individual:

- Real estate is transferred by quitclaim deed.

- Personal property is transferred by bill of sale.

- Stocks, bonds and other investments are transferred by an assignment of assets, or endorsement and delivery of the ownership certificate.

Here are three key points to keep in mind:

1) Real estate. Will you need permission from lenders to transfer title? Also consider document stamps and other recording costs.

**Highlight**

If the partnership is to have a specific business purpose, then the partnership should contain only those assets necessary to fulfill that function.

2)  Stocks, bonds and mutual funds: Simply call your broker or transfer agent. They usually can handle the paperwork necessary for the transfer with a phone call.

3)  Cars, boats and airplanes: Will you have to pay sales tax? You will also need new registrations.

You will find documents to transfer assets in the forms section of this guide.

NOTE: The limited partnership should only own assets intended or suitable for a business or investment. The partnership should be an income-producing entity. Assets that produce neither current income, anticipated income, nor appreciation should not be titled in the partnership. Their inclusion may jeopardize the limited liability of the limited partners.

## Obtaining new insurance

Present insurance carried on the asset must be replaced with insurance obtained through the partnership. Check whether you will incur increased premiums or pay a penalty for the early cancellation of your present policy. Review these insurance questions with your insurance agent before you make the transfer.

**Highlight**
Your present insurance carried on the asset must be replaced with insurance through the partnership.

# CHAPTER

# The limited partnership

If you are considering forming a partnership, you are strongly urged to choose a limited partnership over a general partnership. This is especially important if you want to protect the contributions you put into it. But, you say, we just spent several chapters explaining general partnerships; why discuss them at all if you don't recommend them?

The reason is that the general partnership is a much simpler entity to understand, and serves as a clearer example of how partnerships work. And, for a small business venture with not a lot of capital at stake, a general partnership would work just fine. But the best protection, both for you and your assets, comes from forming a limited partnership.

Historically, limited partnerships were created to allow investors to give money to a business (in the hopes of receiving profits from a successful venture) without anyone knowing they were involved—often called the silent partner. Today, being a limited partner no longer needs to remain a secret, but it still can be one of the best ways to pump money into a business without having too many cooks in the kitchen.

## *Limited vs. general partnership*

A limited partnership has one or more general partners and one or more limited partners. The general partners manage the partnership. The limited partners must remain passive and assert absolutely no active role in managing the partnership. Limited partners who refrain from management participation remain free from personal liability for partnership obligations. Their rights as a limited partner compare to the rights of a stockholder, or member of an LLC, including the right:

- to an accounting
- to inspect partnership books
- to obtain important partnership information
- to share partnership income when distributed at the discretion of the general partner
- to share proceeds proportionate to ownership interest upon liquidation of the partnership

A limited partner's liability is limited only to the amount invested. A limited partner incurs none of the liability of a general partner unless the limited partner helps to manage the partnership. Even occasional or minor management participation can render a limited partner liable. Adopting a limited partner's name for the partnership can, for example, make the limited partner liable to creditors who relied upon this representation to extend credit. Thus, to limit liability, a limited partner must avoid all involvement in partnership activities beyond those few specific authorities enumerated in the Partnership Agreement. A limited partner can own or manage a corporation or LLC, which can, in turn, be the general partner. Owning the general partner entity will not create personal liability because it does not constitute management by the limited partner individually.

What authority may a limited partner assert without incurring liability? A limited partner may:

- work as employee of, or independent contractor to, the limited partnership
- work as an employee of, or independent contractor to, the general partner
- vote to amend the Partnership Agreement
- guarantee partnership debts
- vote to dissolve the partnership or sell, lease, exchange or encumber assets outside the ordinary course of business
- vote to change the nature of the business
- vote to remove or appoint a general partner

While a limited partner cannot direct the general partner, a limited partner can provide advisory opinions or recommendations to the general partner. Final decisions, however, must rest with the general partner.

As we have mentioned previously, the major disadvantage of the general partnership is that its partners are jointly and severally liable for

**Highlight**

Adopting a limited partner's name for the partnership can, for example, make the limited partner liable to creditors who relied upon this representation to extend credit.

partnership debts. A general partner in this type of partnership can easily lose personal wealth to satisfy partnership creditors if the business or other general partners individually have insufficient assets to satisfy these obligations. And you can lose your wealth even if your partner created the liability. Therefore, the general partnership extends liability. A general partner's interest can also be seized by the partner's personal creditors.

Conversely, a limited partnership will fully protect the limited partners' assets from partnership debts, and a partnership interest cannot be seized by a partner's personal creditors. The limited partnership is thus both an excellent liability insulator and wealth protector.

## *Forming your partnership*

In many ways, the limited partnership is created and run just as a general partnership is, with a few notable exceptions:

- All partners but one (the general partner) are allowed limited liability.
- A limited partnership must file a Certificate of Limited Partnership with the state.
- Only general partners may have an active role in the running of the business.
- Limited partnerships are governed by the Uniform Limited Partnership Act (ULPA), except in Louisiana.

To form a limited partnership, you need to have at least one partner as a general partner—with complete liability, as in a general partnership—and you may have any number of limited partners. Most limited partners agree to invest a certain amount of money, expect a certain rate of return (either as a percentage of the contribution or of the profits) and the eventual reimbursement of their investment. The amount and timeline of these investments and returns should be clearly outlined in your Certificate and Partnership Agreement.

Keep in mind that, if your business is large enough, there will be state and/or federal regulations regarding who may invest as a limited partner. For most smaller partnerships, however, you will have no problems as long as you abide by the ULPA, otherwise you risk losing the limited liability status of your limited partners.

# *Creating the partnership* ▬▬▬

### *The certificate*

You will file a Certificate of Limited Partnership (also called "Certificate of Organization" or "Registration Statement") with the state, something not required for a general partnership. Most states have specific forms that you must use though some allow you to file your own. If your state does not require a specific form, you can usually use the Partnership Agreement, making sure you include all the points required by your state. Contact your Department of State for the proper forms and the appropriate regulations.

Remember that amendments to your Certificate must be kept up to date. Any time the law requires a change you need to amend the Certificate, and each state may require different amendments be made. Amendments to your Certificate may be required when any of the following occur:

- the partnership name changes
- there is a change in any partner's status
- a partner is added, removed, or interest is transferred
- the amounts of limited partner investments or distributions change
- the nature of the partnership's business changes
- important dates or timelines change
- any other significant change in the running of the partnership occurs

### *The Partnership Agreement*

Your limited partnership's Agreement will be much like that of a general partnership, with the exception of clauses regarding investments and returns (and timelines regarding both), and policies regarding transfer of interest of the limited partners. It should also include an outline of what a limited partner can and cannot do, keeping in mind the requirements of the ULPA. See the forms in this guide for a sample Limited Partnership Agreement.

The Partnership Agreement is usually not publicly recorded. Only the Certificate of Limited Partnership is filed, which must state only the partnership name, its address, resident agent, general partners, and duration.

**Highlight**

Any time the laws require a change you will need to amend the certificate, and each state may have different changes that will merit an amendment.

After these two documents are completed, go through the same steps as with a general partnership: file with the IRS, be sure to file any amendments to either the Certificate or Partnership Agreement with the state, keep your records up-to-date, and take care of business!

## The foreign partnership

If your limited partnership will not actively engage in business in your state, you may want to establish your partnership in another state. Every state except for Louisiana has adopted the Uniform Limited Partnership Act, so laws concerning limited partnerships are generally the same. Local taxation issues and filing fees will influence you as to which state to register in. You can expect to pay between $1,500 and $5,000 to form a customized limited partnership.

## The limited partner

The general partner in a limited partnership is just like a partner in a general partnership. The limited partner, however, plays a different role. As we mentioned earlier, the limited partner invests in the business and receives returns on his or her investment, yet has only a passive role in the running of the business. A limited partner cannot receive partnership property or hold partnership property as collateral or security for any reason. And a limited partner cannot expect distributions if the partnership is insolvent or is unable to pay past due debts.

What a limited partner can do, however, is do business with the partnership, as well as act as consultant to the general partner. A limited partner may also compete directly with the business of the partnership! This can—and does—happen, but if you wish, you may write a provision in your Partnership Agreement prohibiting this. In fact, you may define the role of the limited partner in your Partnership Agreement any way at all, keeping in mind that rejecting ULPA guidelines could result in the loss of limited liability. In general, it is best to keep the limited partner's role in the business as passive as possible.

Who makes the best limited partner? For the average small business, your best bets are close friends and family. The reason is that, as a small, start-up business with little or no track record, banks and other lenders will likely not take a chance on lending you money to get your company off the ground, and private investors may not know you well enough to gamble their money on you running the show. Theoretically, anyone at all can be a limited partner, as long as they have the money to invest.

**Highlight**

If your limited partnership will not actively engage in business in your state, you may establish your partnership in another state. Local taxation issues and filing fees will influence you as to which state to register in.

You need to realize, though, that as an investment a limited partnership is considered a security—and therefore the investment is subject to state and/or federal regulations. To be exempt from federal regulations, you need only to limit your sale of interests in the limited partnership to people within your state. To be exempt from state regulations, however, or to be exempt from federal regulations on an interstate sale, you need to make what is called a "private offering" (as opposed to a public offering). Every state has specific guidelines for what it considers a private offering, but generally it means the interests are offered to a specified number of people (usually no more than 35 people). Some states may have other restrictions, so if you aren't sure if your sale will qualify as a private offering, contact the appropriate state department (often the Secretary of State's office) and be sure to consult an attorney when drawing up your Limited Partnership Certificate and Partnership Agreement.

## Asset protection and the limited partnership

A growing number of people are forming limited partnerships as a form of asset protection, which is a means of legally preventing the attachment of your assets by creditors and others. The primary advantage of a limited partnership—limited liability—means not being liable for debts of the partnership. The assets invested in a limited partnership by a limited partner facing bankruptcy or anxious creditors cannot be reached by those creditors, provided that the assets weren't invested in the partnership solely for the sake of protecting them. And the partnership is protected from any individual partner's creditors as well.

In order to maintain this protection, you must make certain you run a legitimate partnership. Creditors can ignore your partnership or hold you personally liable for monies or other assets removed from the partnership if you personally or improperly use the partnership or its assets. The partnership, as with a corporation or LLC, must be treated as an arms-length and independent entity.

The partnership must maintain its own bank accounts, separate books and records, insurance, licenses and permits, and employer identification number. Its cash and other assets must also remain separated from assets of other entities or individuals and never commingled. If you should use partnership assets for personal use, then pay fair compensation. Loans to or borrowing from the partnership must be properly documented. Respect the

**Highlight**

The assets invested in a limited partnership by a limited partner facing bankruptcy or anxious creditors cannot be reached by those creditors, provided that the assets weren't invested solely for the sake of protecting them.

independent status of the partnership if you expect it to protect you.

### *How limited partnerships protect assets*

Limited partnership law balances the rights of a partner's creditors against the rights of the non-debtor partners who want to remain free from creditor interference in their partnership dealings. Because one partner has financial problems, it should not impede other partners. Thus a limited partner's personal creditors are severely limited in remedies against the debtor-partner's interest in the limited partnership.

A creditor in this case can only apply to the court for a charging order. This gives the creditor only the right to receive the profits distributed from the partnership to the debtor-partner. However, the creditor can seize neither the debtor-partner's partnership interest nor partnership property because the partners collectively share the partnership property as tenants-in-partnership. Since the partnership property does not legally belong to any individual partner, it therefore cannot be taken by any personal creditors of an individual debtor-partner. Property transferred to the partnership is thus safe from a partner's future creditors. Key assets can be protected from litigation and other claims by titling those assets in the partnership name. Equipment, intellectual property (trademarks, copyrights, patents) and real estate are frequently owned by a limited partnership. The business entity would then lease or license these assets from the partnership while the business uses the assets. Partnership ownership thus protects these assets from a business bankruptcy.

The ULPA limits a creditor to this charging order remedy. A creditor who seeks relief against a limited partner can neither dissolve the limited partnership nor interfere with partnership activities. The debtor-partner's personal creditor, in essence, becomes only an assignee of the partnership interest. The creditor gains only the right to receive the debtor-partner's profit distributions if and when paid, and only to the extent of the debt.

Limited Partnership Agreements generally forbid a partner's creditor from becoming a full limited partner. Thus the creditor-assignee acquires no voice in partnership management or voting. A creditor-assignee cannot acquire rights in the partnership above those possessed by the limited partner. And a limited partner's rights are generally restricted only to receiving income. Thus, the creditor-assignee's charging order remedy is nearly worthless because the general partner alone determines profit distributions. And, for good measure, a well-drafted Partnership Agreement forbids an assignee (e.g., a partner's creditor) from becoming a limited

**Highlight**

A creditor who seeks relief against a limited partner can neither dissolve the limited partnership nor interfere with partnership activities. The creditor gains only the right to receive the debtor-partner's profit distributions if and when paid, and to the extent of their debt.

partner without the consent of all partners. It also allows the general partner to withhold profit distributions from limited partners for legitimate business purposes.

Therefore, the general partner may refuse to issue dividends to limited partners. Of course, the general partner can withdraw income or funds from the partnership for wages, fees, loans, to transact business with affiliated entities or for a variety of other legitimate reasons. If more than one creditor has a charging order, the first creditor to apply for the charging order obtains priority. An individual partner's creditor has no priority over partnership creditors. If no assets remain once partnership creditors are paid, the individual partner's creditors receive nothing from the partnership.

A properly drafted partnership thus gives a partner's creditors no practical recourse other than to await an income distribution that the creditor can neither force nor anticipate. This explains why the partnership is one of the most popular domestic asset protection tools.

CHAPTER

# The family limited partnership

When you hear the term family partnership, you probably think of a family-run business, something like a company called "Joe Smith and Sons." But a family partnership is much more complex, and it most likely has nothing to do with a business at all. Most often, a family will create a limited partnership to protect the family's assets, and it also can prove to be a valuable tool in estate planning.

## *History of the family limited partnership* ■

Until the 1986 Tax Reform Act, limited partnerships were formed as tax shelter structures that only wealthy investors seeking tax losses could make use of, but a family could also form a partnership provided it met the right conditions. At that time, the family partnership was the best way for a family of moderate wealth to reap the benefits of partnership taxation and keep the money all in the family.

The tax shelter benefits for the wealthy investors disappeared with the Tax Reform Act of 1986, and the distinction of the family partnership was no longer necessary. Today, a family partnership is simply a regular limited partnership that chooses to keep its partners within the family. It can be a great way to maintain and protect a family's wealth, as long as you structure it following sound advice from tax and financial advisors.

Partners in a limited partnership may allocate their ownership interest as they choose, and this is an important feature for asset protection purposes. For instance, you may contribute personal assets to the partnership and obtain in exchange only a small partnership interest. The remaining partnership interest may be owned by other family members.

However, this arrangement can create a taxable gift when the other family member is not your spouse. For example, if you contribute $100,000 to the limited partnership and your partner contributes nothing but receives an equal share, then your partner effectively receives a $50,000 gift.

## *Structure of a family limited partnership* ▪

There are typical limited partnership structures for families. Since a family partnership is often used for estate planning, the most common setup features parents contributing most of the assets and children receiving the largest interest and profit.

Most often, mom and dad form the partnership, contributing various income-producing or business assets in exchange for their respective partnership interests. They can receive a small percent interest in the partnership as the general partners, and as such would equally control the partnership the same way they controlled the contributed assets before. Mom and dad may each also receive, as limited partners, the remaining majority interest in the limited partnership (general and limited partners can be the same parties and both can own an interest in a limited partnership). This allows mom and dad exclusive, equal ownership and control of the partnership—and thus the assets they contributed to the partnership—just as they had enjoyed when their assets were titled in their own names. The one difference is that their assets are now fully protected from creditors.

There are many other ways to structure a family partnership. Perhaps dad has a lot of creditors and only mom becomes the general partner. It would not be to dad's advantage to be a general partner, with full liability in the partnership, where those creditors could then come after partnership assets. Another approach is for mom and dad to form a corporation or LLC which would be the general partner in the partnership. This is a particularly good choice if the partnership can incur liabilities for which the general partner(s) is liable.

Mom and dad may subsequently alter their limited partnership interests. Or they may gradually gift their limited partnership interests to their children, or to a living trust or other entity, which may also own a portion of the limited partnership. Since the limited partnership's structure is never permanent, the family limited partnership works very well for estate planning.

**Highlight**

Since the limited partnership's structure is never permanent, the family limited partnership can work very well for estate planning.

# *Three advantages to the family limited partnership*

### 1) The family limited partnership as financial planner.

In a society where a volatile economy and the rate of divorce can make any family's financial picture unstable, the family limited partnership is likely to become more and more popular, and for more than mere estate planning. The family limited partnership can become a useful tool for organizing your long-term family finances while offering the bonus of protecting the money you have, whether you want to save for your kids' futures or prepare for your golden years. The key advantage with the family limited partnership is that you keep control of your assets.

The greatest financial concern of any parent is being able to set aside money for their child's future: college, a wedding, their first home, etc. Investing money is not only smart but crucial. But what happens when you take the money you've accumulated and give it to your children, only to find them spending the college tuition on a custom sports car? Or when your child's marriage ends in divorce and the money *you* worked so hard to make ends up in the ex-spouse's pocket?

Many parents are able to give money to their children through the Uniform Transfer to Minors Act, where the parents act as custodian of the money they set aside. The problem here is that the parents lose control when the child turns 21, so the child *can* take the college tuition and squander it on a regrettable purchase—and one you'll be unable to correct. With a family limited partnership, however, you can give your children the same amount of money without ever losing control of the assets, assuring that your children are provided for in the manner you expect them to be.

### 2) The divorce safety net

With the divorce rate still hovering at 50%, you need to be even more concerned with the money you give your child. Lets say you gift your only son with the family home, a historically significant and treasured piece of real estate upon which your great-grandfather built a tremendous edifice one hundred years ago. Then your son marries a nice girl, they have two children, and six years later divorce. Your son's ex-wife gets the family home, and your family has lost a priceless part of its heritage.

With a family limited partnership, you can keep family property and money in the family's control by transferring it to the partnership—which

Highlight

The family limited partnership can become a useful tool for organizing your long-term family finances while offering the bonus of protection the money you have, whether you want to save for your kids' futures or prepare for your golden years.

you control as general partner. You may then give your children limited partner interests which remain with the partnership (and thus, your family) no matter how many creditors or ex-spouses come after the limited partners. Even if you just want to give your children money, you could have the partnership loan them the money instead, so the funds could not be attached by a creditor or through a divorce.

In addition to children, this method may protect your grandchildren as well. In the above example, any money you had given to your son's two children could then be commingled and divided in the divorce, so your son's ex-wife not only receives the family property but also all the gifts you gave your grandchildren. Again, giving your grandchildren limited partner interests could prevent that from happening, keep the money in the family, and ensure that your grandchildren are provided for.

A warning: As mentioned before, a family limited partnership may greatly benefit a family by protecting against the loss of assets if assigned to the partnership, but beware of the old divorce trick. There was a time when a soon-to-be-divorced husband would form a limited partnership, naming his soon-to-be ex-wife as limited partner. Upon divorce, the settlement would give the wife, as limited partner, half the assets of the partnership but no control, and no cash settlement. Without any money, she would have to settle for selling her interest to the ex-husband at a substantially low price, leaving her with only a small amount of money. Fortunately, this doesn't happen often anymore, as judges and divorce attorneys (and now you) are wise to this scheme.

### 3) Tax benefits

The greatest advantage of a partnership over other business entities is the pass-through tax status a partnership enjoys, and a limited partnership allows for even greater tax flexibility. Though families choose the limited partnership mainly to keep control of and protect family assets, the tax benefits are equally as advantageous.

The most common tax feature utilized in the family limited partnership is the ability to spread the tax burden between the partners any way you choose. For example, a general partner (Dad) with a high tax bracket could contribute a large amount of money to a partnership where he has only a small percent interest in the partnership (but all the control). The tax burden for this contribution would be spread to the limited partners (the kids), who have the majority of interests in the partnership as well as being in a low tax bracket. Dad, in fact, can continue to contribute and thus spread

**Highlight**

Giving your grandchildren limited partner interests could keep the money in the family, and ensure your grandchildren are provided for.

the tax burden until it no longer saves him taxes—which, theoretically, might never occur.

## Assets for a family limited partnership ■■

The family limited partnership should generally not own the family residence unless the property is held for investment purposes. Several tax disadvantages also arise from titling the family home to a limited partnership. Collectibles, such as jewelry, coins and antiques, are appropriate for a partnership if their value is expected to increase. A partnership cannot own shares in an S corporation but can own interest in an LLC. IRA and other retirement accounts cannot be owned by a partnership. Annuities may be owned, but you would then lose their tax deferral benefits. Autos and boats should not be owned by the partnership unless they are used in connection with a business.

Should you wish to form a family limited partnership, it is best to consult with your attorney and tax advisor, to ensure you comply with all tax regulations and make the most of contributed assets.

## Combining with trusts for extra protection ■■■■

A trust is a legal agreement in which a person owning property, called the grantor (or principal, settlor or donor), hands over legal title to his or her property to a second person, called the trustee, who manages it for the grantor. As grantor, you do not give up the right to use or sell the property; it is simply put in another person's name so as to avoid federal estate taxes and probate when you die. The trustee has the power to buy, sell, lease, or invest property according to your instructions, but you have final say as to what happens to all trust property. With most trusts, you may end the trust agreement or appoint a different trustee at any time. Property may be added to or taken out of the trust as needed.

Like the general partner of a limited partnership, as grantor you remain in control of your property. You may choose your spouse, a relative, close friend, or knowledgeable financial advisor or attorney to serve as trustee of your trust, or you may also serve as your own trustee (only New York requires you to appoint a co-trustee). Even if you are your own trustee, your assets are protected from probate, since legally they are owned by the trust, a separate entity, rather than by you.

**Highlight**
The family limited partnership should generally not own the family residence unless the property is held for investment purposes. Several tax disadvantages also arise from titling the family home to a limited partnership.

The joining of these two strategies could make for a powerful family asset protector. However, because combining trusts with a limited partnership is much more complicated than using either one by itself, you should seek out the legal and financial counsel necessary to make the most of them and to protect your family's assets.

Combining trusts with a family limited partnership can offer even greater protection, since you can further frustrate creditors from seizing limited partnership interests by having a foreign asset protection trust own the limited partnership interest. Set up in this manner, a foreign asset protection trust usually serves as the sole limited partner and owns almost 100% of the partnership. There is also a type of trust called a "defective trust" which can be used for tax purposes when the general partner is in a lower tax bracket than the limited partners (unlike the typical family partnership). Again, The creation of a foreign or defective trust—or any type of trust—in conjunction with a family limited partnership is complicated, especially regarding tax matters, and should always be attempted with sound legal and financial advice.

# CHAPTER 8

# The limited liability partnership

Every doctor, lawyer or other professional carries insurance against malpractice and other types of litigation; claims against these professionals are a daily occurrence. But no professional today can rely solely upon insurance for protection. There are now many other opportunities for professionals to incur liability arising from their practice. The need for sound organizational protection for professionals clearly matches that of the commercial business owner.

Enter the limited liability partnership. This is a special kind of partnership created for those engaged in professional occupations such as doctors, lawyers, dentists, architects and accountants. It is called a limited liability partnership, or LLP, because it bears a great resemblance to the limited partnership, though there are important differences between the two.

## *Why form an LLP?*

The single biggest concern for a business involved in fields such as the medical or legal profession is the threat of malpractice. If your average partnership is concerned with the attachment of company assets by company creditors, a professional business is concerned a hundred times over. In these modern times, it is commonplace for a doctor or lawyer to be sued for any number of reasons; in fact, these professionals expect it. That is why most of them carry malpractice insurance, and why forming a limited liability partnership can offer them significant protection.

While the LLP protects the professional partner from debts incurred by the practice, as well as claims resulting from the malpractice of any other partner, it does not protect the professional partner from claims resulting from his/her own malpractice. Moreover, the LLP's assets cannot be directly seized by the professional partner's personal creditors. Nor can the professional partner's personal creditors easily liquidate his/her interest in the LLP, because interest in this type of partnership must be owned by professionals from within that profession. This makes the LLP an excellent option when professionals want to participate in the management of the practice while insulating personal assets from the partnership liabilities.

## How the LLP works

A limited liability partnership shares common features with these other types of partnerships. Like a general partnership, all partners in an LLP are liable for commercial debts and other partnership actions. However, when a partner is held responsible for malpractice—or anyone under his direct supervision is held responsible—only that partner is held liable. The remainder of the partners are shielded from any liability incurred by the professional misconduct of one partner. Most states which have adopted the Revised Uniform Partnership Act have extended that shield to cover not only tort claims but contract claims as well.

Despite the continued liability of partners for partnership debts, and personal liability if sued for malpractice, the LLP is a wise choice for professionals since no partner is held liable for another partner's inappropriate or negligent practice of that profession. This allows for high risk professions to reap the benefits of forming a partnership without sacrificing a career because of another's mistakes.

## Things to keep in mind

The professionals' asset protection improves when they conduct their practice through an LLP. Conversely, the general partnership is the most dangerous business structure because each partner then has unlimited liability for all partnership debts. Should you still want the general partnership, each professional operating as a partner in the general partnership should, at the least, organize his/her own professional corporation or LLC. The respective entities could then become partners in the partnership.

While this creates a somewhat more cumbersome arrangement than with an LLP, the structure provides certain tax, regulatory or organizational advantages. In a general partnership, the partners are all equally liable for partnership debts. In exchange, the partners enjoy the

**Highlight**

The LLP is a wise choice for professionals since no partner is held liable for another partner's inappropriate or negligent practice of that profession. This allows for high risk professions to reap the benefits of forming a partnership without sacrificing a career over another's mistakes.

pass-through tax benefits not found in a corporation. In a limited partnership, all partners except one have limited liability; that one general partner is personally liable for any and all partnership debts.

Remember, an LLP helps minimize the risk of its partners, but nothing can completely eliminate that risk. And don't mistakenly think you no longer need malpractice insurance if you form an LLP. Carefully consider taxes, state regulations for your profession, and malpractice insurance when creating your LLP Agreement.

# CHAPTER

# Taxes and
# the partnership

S corporations, living trusts and limited partnerships are all pass-through entities because they allocate income, deductions, gains and losses directly to each stockholder, grantor or partner in proportion to their ownership interest. The partnership similarly files a partnership tax return but pays no tax on its own earnings. Instead, the partnership completes IRS form K-1, reporting profits and losses attributable and reportable to each partner. Partners are responsible for reporting those profits and losses on their individual tax returns. The partnership is thus tax-neutral and itself presents no tax disadvantages.

Like S corporations and some LLCs, partnerships have their profits taxed only once: partners or stockholders pay an income tax on their proportionate share of the partnership income whether or not any profits were received. C corporation profits, however, are taxed twice: once when earned by the corporation and again when distributed as dividend income to the shareholders. This is the single biggest advantage of a partnership.

When assets are transferred to the partnership, it is not a taxable event. The partnership accepts the assets at the transferor's cost. The partnership, when it sells its assets, assumes the transferor's loss or gain.

## *Taxation of partnership income*

Partnerships are not taxpayers; nevertheless they must determine taxable income. Partnership income is computed then as it is for individuals except deductions are not allowed for personal exemptions, foreign taxes, net operating loss carrybacks and carryovers, charitable contributions, itemized deductions, capital loss carryovers, or depletion deductions.

The partnership itself pays no income tax. The partners pay the taxes on partnership income even if the income is not actually distributed to the partners. This remains true even when the partners cannot withdraw their shares but must retain them in the partnership as capital.

The partnership agreement largely controls the allocation of taxable income or losses, or any other income item, gain, loss, deduction or credit. A partner for only part of the year is allocated only a portion of the taxable income. Tax allocations are based on the ratio used to set a partner's share of profits or losses from business operations.

## Reporting of partnership income

While a limited partnership is not taxed on its profits or other income and gains, this does not mean that partnership income is tax-free. The partnership must file an annual information return that identifies the partnership's income or loss, as well as other income and deductions directly allocated to the partners. This information is reported to the IRS on Form 1065.

This requirement ensures that each partner accurately claims shares of partnership income and deductions on their tax returns. Partners must include on their individual tax returns all income, deductions, credit and loss items passed through from the partnership. Partnership returns must be filed beginning in the first year the partnership has income and deductions. Thereafter the IRS will expect a Form 1065 annually, even if the partnership has no reportable income. At least one partner must sign the return ensuring its accuracy.

## Filing tax returns

Most partnerships operate on a calendar year rather than a fiscal year. In general, the taxable year from the partnership must coincide with the taxable year of one or more partners whose combined interest in partnership profits and capital exceeds 50 percent. Otherwise, the partnership tax year must be the tax year of all the principal partners of the partnership. If all the principal partners do not have the same taxable year, the partnership's taxable year generally becomes the calendar year. A principal partner is one who has more than a 5 percent interest in the partnership capital or profits. A partnership may elect a noncalendar taxable year if it has a valid business purpose for doing so. Calendar year partnerships must file Form 1065 on or before April 15 after each partnership's taxable year. If the partnership

**Highlight**

The partnership must file an annual information return that identifies the partnership's income or loss, as well as other income and deductions directly allocated to the partners. This requirement ensures that each partner accurately claim their shares of partnership income and deductions on their tax returns.

needs additional time to file, it has an automatic extension—not to exceed three months.

Form 1065 is not solely a tax form because it also provides information to the IRS about the partnership. Additional schedules to fill out are:

- Schedule A of form 1065 is used by the partnership to report its income. The company lists the value of its inventory and the method it used to compute that value.

- A partnership must also file Schedule K-1 which shows earned profit distributions. This form provides the IRS with information about a partner's income from the partnership.

- Schedule L reports the company's balance sheet

- Schedule D reports long-term and short-term capital gains and losses.

There may be additional schedules to file along with form 1065 if the partnership has:

- total gross receipts above $250,000

- total assets above $600,000

Generally, every partnership has a choice of accounting methods. The two accepted methods are:

1) Cash. The cash accounting method derives company income from cash or property when actually received.

2) Accrual. The accrual method states that income is derived when the company receives the right to receive the cash or property.

While smaller partnerships generally use the cash method of accounting, the IRS requires the accrual method under two conditions:

1) If a C corporation with average annual income in excess of $5 million is a partner of the partnership

2) If the IRS determines the partnership to be a tax shelter.

Failure to file the partnership or to include the mandatory information imposes a late penalty not to exceed $50 per month per partner. This penalty can accumulate for five months. When the failure to file a complete and timely return is due to "good cause," the IRS may waive the penalty.

The partnership also becomes subject to penalties if it does not furnish copies of K-1 Schedules (part of Form 1065) to each partner. If the

**Highlight**

Generally, every partnership has a choice of accounting methods: cash and accrual. While smaller partnerships generally use the cash method of accounting, the IRS requires the accrual method under certain conditions.

noncompliance is due to "reasonable cause" rather than willful negligence, the IRS may waive the penalty. The K-1 is the reporting part of the partnership return that attributes proportionate income and expenses to each partner and the K-1 is used by the IRS to monitor proper reporting of partnership income.

## *Partnership contributions*

Partnerships, like all businesses, need capital to operate. Capital comes through contributions from partners in exchange for their interests in the partnership. Contributions may be money, property or services. When property is contributed, the partner is credited with the property's fair market value at the time of contribution.

Contributions of cash or property only establish the partner's initial tax basis in the partnership. The partners are only changing the nature of their assets from cash or property to a partnership interest and neither a gain nor a loss is realized. Transferring assets to a partnership will not then create a taxable event for the contributing partners, regardless of whether the partnership is newly created or an existing one.

Services exchanged for a partnership interest follow a different rule because services rendered, or to be rendered, are not considered "property." The partnership interest given in exchange for services to the partnership is seen as compensation, or ordinary income, received from the partnership. Since the interest is then seen as income, this type of exchange is considered a taxable event.

The above refers to services exchanged for an ownership interest in the partnership. However, if the services offered are only in exchange for profits from the partnership (such as with a limited partner), than contributing the services is not a taxable event; the partner is then taxed only upon receiving profits.

An existing partnership interest purchased from another partner, rather than the partnership, does not fall under this rule. These purchases are considered the same as purchasing any other type of property. The purchasing partner's initial cost is equal to what he or she pays for the interest, plus the selling partner's share of partnership debts, since these debts must be assumed by the purchasing partner.

**Highlight**

Contributions of cash or property only establish the partner's initial tax basis in the partnership. The partners are only changing the nature of their assets from cash or property to a partnership interest and neither a gain nor a loss is realized.

## *Tax basis* ▰▰▰▰▰▰▰▰▰▰▰

In order for a partner's tax to be calculated, he or she must first figure out how much the interest in the partnership is worth. This initial amount, or tax basis, is the starting point in calculating the income tax of a partner.

The partner's cost of an interest in a limited partnership depends on the contributed property. If it is money, the partner's cost is the amount of money contributed. If the partner contributes property, the cost of the partner's interest is the cost of the property at the time of contribution. If property transferred to the partnership is subject to debts or mortgages, the partner's cost is reduced by the indebtedness assumed by the partnership.

Partnership distributions are usually made at the end of the partnership year. These distributions may be taxed only when the partner's cash distribution exceeds the cost of his interest in the partnership.

Increases to the partner's tax basis include his distributive share of partnership taxable income, pro rata share of life insurance proceeds, partnership tax exempt income and excess depletion deductions on mineral rights. Distributable partnership taxable income is usually profits from the partnership business and such other partnership income as interest, rents, dividends, royalties and capital gains.

A different approach is used when a partner obtains a partnership interest by gift or inheritance. The cost of the gifted partnership interest equals the cost to the gifting partner. Conversely, inherited partnership interests have a "step up" basis. The inheriting partner's cost equals the fair market value of the interest at the time of the deceased partner's death, or another specified date.

What is the cost of property contributed to the partnership? A partner transfers the cost of his contributed property to the partnership. The partnership thus has the same cost in contributed property as if the property remained owned by the partner. But nonbusiness property may not be entitled to this transfer cost treatment. If a partner contributes nonbusiness property such as a personal residence or automobile to the partnership, the cost of the property to the partnership becomes the fair market value of the property when it was contributed, or the cost to the contributing partner, whichever is higher. For tax purposes, the partnership is allowed to depreciate nonbusiness assets, even if the contributing partner claimed the depreciation.

## *Partnerships and estate taxes*

Assets in a limited partnership may have a discounted value of 20 to 40 percent for gift and estate tax valuations. The discount will depend on the control over the partnership and the liquidity, marketability and accessibility of its assets. Discounting the value is a topic under constant IRS review, with the rules subject to change.

## *Partnership tax qualifications*

If you seek partnership classification for tax purposes, it is important to follow IRS guidelines, lest you be taxed as a corporation or association.

Partnerships must possess certain characteristics to qualify as a business entity that should be taxed by the IRS as a pass-through partnership. Failure to qualify may result in classification as an association, which is taxed as a corporation. Both partnerships and corporations have associates, a business objective and the intent to divide the profits. Unique characteristics of a corporation include centralized management, continuous life, liability for corporate debts limited to the corporation, and free transferability of shares.

How the IRS taxes the business entity depends upon whether the entity exhibits more corporate than non-corporate characteristics. If a partnership has equal or less corporate and non-corporate characteristics, the entity is considered a limited partnership for tax purposes. Therefore, a limited partnership with both centralized management and unrestricted transferability of interests but without continuous life and limited liability should not be taxed as a corporation. If you adhere to the common provisions found in standard limited partnership agreements, then you have little danger the IRS will disqualify the partnership status.

It is possible to obtain an IRS ruling on your partnership by mail. Although the procedure is complicated and expensive, you can resolve any doubts you have about the status of your partnership. Such a ruling gives your company the opportunity to comply before serious tax liability is incurred. The fee for a Private Letter Ruling is about $500. It is based solely upon the information your company provides and applies only to your company. It does not address the partnership laws in your state. You must not use prior rulings as a guide.

**Highlight**

The IRS examines several characteristics to determine whether the entity should be taxed as a pass-through partnership or as an association and thus taxes as a corporation.

# *Partnership tax cautions* ▬▬

- The combined interests of all general partners must equal at least one percent of the operating income and losses, as well as capital gains and losses.

- Distributions to limited and general partners may be in any desired proportion and need not coincide with either the amount each partner invested or his/her percentage ownership. This can be a great advantage in asset protection or estate planning. You may, for example, agree to accept less income from your greater share in the partnership, while other partners (such as family members) with a lesser interest may receive disproportionately greater income.

- A partner's share of partnership operating losses as a deduction on his/her personal return is limited by the "at risk" provisions of the IRS code. This limits the deductibility of a partner's share of any loss to the amount the partner actually invested, or what the partner could potentially lose from the partnership.

- It is important to remember that the limited partnership can lose its pass-through tax advantage and be taxed as a C corporation if the partnership violates state laws. Its tax benefits can also be lost when the limited partnership has a corporation as its general partner and fewer assets than liabilities. To avoid losing single taxation status, the limited partnership should have at least one unincorporated general partner. The primary reason a corporation would be used as a general partner is to avoid personal liability for partnership debts, but this is only a necessary precaution when the partnership engages in liability-incurring activity. If the limited partnership holds and manages only safe, passive assets, then risk is no longer an issue and individuals can safely serve as general partners.

## *Highlight*

Taxation of the entity depends upon whether it features more corporate than non-corporate characteristics. If a partnership has equal corporate and non-corporate characteristics, the entity is considered a limited partnership for tax purposes.

# *Other considerations* ▬▬

### *Start-up costs*

The expenses you incur while starting up your business—before the partnership actually is formed, but which are essential to forming the partnership and getting your business off the ground—are called capital expenditures. It is important to remember that you can deduct these expenses when figuring your taxes. However, the IRS doesn't allow you to deduct it all at once. The value of your capital expenditures is spread over a period of time, which is called "amortization." The IRS requires a partnership to amortize over a period of 60 months, so, even though it may not seem like much of a deduction each year, deducting these expenses will benefit you over the long term.

### *Getting help*

We can't stress enough the importance of using a good accountant and/or tax specialist. Even if your business is very small, it is easy to mess up the books or err on your taxes, and the IRS won't be very sympathetic. Since you'll have significant issues to deal with such as choosing a tax year, deciding whether to pay estimated tax, dealing with deductions for business expenses, and handling employee accounts, you must choose your accountant/tax advisor carefully. To help you choose a good accountant or tax advisor, you can use many of the hints and guidelines used for selecting an attorney found in the *How To Save On Attorney Fees* bonus section later in this guide.

The taxation of a business is a complicated matter, and this chapter has only outlined the basics of the tax laws that concern partnerships. Since we cannot possibly address all the issues involved, and you are urged to seek the help of accountants, tax specialists and other qualified professionals.

**Highlight**

It is important to remember that you can deduct capital expenditures when figuring your taxes. However, the IRS doesn't allow you to deduct it all at once.

# CHAPTER

# Dissolving your partnership

There are two general ways to dissolve a partnership: by voluntary or involuntary dissolution. Voluntary dissolution involves action taken by the partnership according to provisions established in the Partnership Agreement. Involuntary dissolution occurs by operation of law.

## *Involuntary dissolution*

This occurs when the court orders the dissolution of a partnership, for one of several reasons. For example, a court may order dissolution for:

- non-payment of taxes
- failure to maintain a registered agent or registered office
- partnership misconduct
- failure of the partnership to return a partnership contribution to a member
- completely merging with another firm
- disqualifying business activities (for example, a partnership cannot become a banking, financial or insurance institution)
- failure to file required reports or pay state fees

## *Voluntary dissolution*

A voluntary dissolution can occur by *expiration*, *partnership withdrawal* or *agreement*.

1) **Expiration.** This occurs when the expiration date of the partnership as set forth in the Partnership Agreement has been

reached. This is usually 30 years from the date of formation, although a longer duration is allowed.

Instead of a fixed date, expiration may result from the occurrence of a specific event. This is known as a "contingent expiration" and must also be included in the initial filings of the partnership. Dissolution by expiration is necessary in order that the partnership avoid having continuity of life, which could jeopardize the tax status of the partnership.

2) **Withdrawal.** This dissolution usually occurs in accordance with state law, when a partner withdraws from the partnership. While it may be a voluntary withdrawal, such as in retirement or bankruptcy, it also may be involuntary as when a partner is expelled, dies or becomes incapacitated. Even if a partner's withdrawal is not legal, the effect of dissolution is the same. The partner, however, may be subject to legal action for the wrongful act.

Note: The trend in some UPA governed states is to allow a partner to voluntarily withdraw without triggering dissolution. (Under the RUPA, withdrawal of a partner does not automatically trigger dissolution.) This is allowed if prior notice is given (usually at least 30 days) and is allowed even if it conflicts with provisions in the Partnership Agreement.

In the event withdrawal of a partner triggers dissolution, the partnership may continue to exist in one of two ways:

1) The Partnership Agreement may so state that the partnership should continue to exist. This is called *continuation by prior agreement*. If your state allows this type agreement, it is the preferred method. It effectively prevents a partner who may lack the voting power to do so from destroying the partnership.

2) In the absence of such a provision, the remaining partners may consent to continue the partnership. This usually requires a vote. Some states require a unanimous vote of the membership while others only a majority vote. Regardless of what type of vote an individual state requires, check the current IRS ruling on voting requirements, as it may differ.

**Highlight**

Dissolution by expiration is necessary in order that the partnership avoid having continuity of life, which could jeopardize the tax status of the partnership.

No one wants something successful and beneficial to end. If you plan your limited partnership right, it should not end, at least not before you and your partners are ready to dissolve it.

# The termination process

The termination process itself is fairly simple, and there are endless situations under which a termination can occur. Sometimes one or two partners want out of the partnership while other partners want to continue on. Sometimes partners may want to expel a particularly troublesome partner. Some examples:

**Highlight**

Once partners prepare to leave or the partnership appears positioned for termination, all partners should discuss and negotiate a special Separation Agreement.

- Partner X, a solid businessman when he joined the partnership, drinks excessively, embarrassing the other partners, making it difficult to conduct business.

- Partner Y has stolen partnership funds. The remaining partners want to file criminal charges against him and expel him from the partnership.

- Partners A and B want to leave the partnership. The two remaining partners, C and D, want to continue. Only C is solvent.

- Partner E just celebrated his 90th birthday and wants to sell his partnership interest and retire to the Bahamas. However, he is worried about the income tax he may be assessed upon the sale of his interest.

## The Separation Agreement

You can't always foresee circumstances that will lead to the termination of a partners' involvement or of the partnership itself. So it isn't always advisable to state rigid termination requirements in your Partnership Agreement. Instead, once partners prepare to leave or the partnership appears positioned for termination, all partners should discuss and negotiate a special Separation Agreement. This Separation Agreement should minimally contain these five points:

1) which partners will retain specific partnership assets

2) who will notify clients and creditors of the termination

3) whether income distributions to the departing partners will be in a lump sum or in installments

4) how taxes on such distributions will be allocated and paid

5) how partnership debts will be resolved

The two most common scenarios concerning partnership terminations are:

1) one or more partners either want out or must be expelled and the partnership is to continue

2) all or a majority of partners leave and the partnership entity ends

How you handle the first situation depends on why the partner is leaving. If a voluntary departure, it will be simple enough to sit down with that partner and arrange to purchase his interest. However, if you are expelling a partner for cause, such as incompetence, bankruptcy or illegal behavior, you may need to negotiate through attorneys.

### The buy-out clause

Several essential clauses should be in your Partnership Agreement concerning the "buy out" of a partner.

- First, the agreement should clearly state that if partners owning a majority interest leave, the partnership continues with the remaining partners. Without such a clause, the partnership may be forced into dissolution upon any one partner's withdrawal.

- Second, the Agreement should require withdrawing partners to give adequate notice of withdrawal or face penalties. One possible penalty is to reduce the partnership interest. The remaining partners should also have a right of first refusal, and be offered the withdrawing partner's interest before the shares are offered to outsiders. This ensures that the partnership belongs, if they desire, to the existing partners. The Agreement should further specify that if the shares are offered to outsiders, the majority of the remaining partners must consent before the outsider may join the partnership as a full partner. This ensures that the partnership does not have to accept undesirable outsiders as full partners.

Unless the Partnership Agreement states otherwise, withdrawing partners remain responsible for outstanding liabilities they owe the partnership. The remaining partners may agree to pay these liabilities as part of the buyout agreement.

### Distributing partner interests

Another issue raised by a withdrawing partner is how that partner will receive payment for his or her interest. RUPA states have a set formula, but for UPA states, there are several ways to value a partnership interest:

**Highlight**

Unless the Partnership Agreement states otherwise, withdrawing partners remain responsible for outstanding liabilities they owe the partnership, unless the remaining partners agree to pay these liabilities as part of the buyout agreement.

1) **Buyout Clauses**: A clause may be included in the Partnership or Separation Agreement, requiring a professional appraiser value the withdrawing partner's interest. A buyout price can also be negotiated with the withdrawing partners. Remaining partners should obtain separate appraisals.

2) **Asset-Value Method**: This calculates present net worth of the partnership, subtracting liabilities from assets. This net worth should include all intangible assets, as well as accounts receivable, and cash. The withdrawing partner receives the percentage of the net worth proportionate to his or her partnership interest.

3) **Fixed Method**: Alternatively, all partners may periodically agree in advance to pay withdrawing partners a fixed price, regardless of the partnership's net worth at the time of withdrawal. This avoids complicated formulas or professional appraisals.

4) **Time of Departure Method**: The agreement may give the partner withdrawing the amount contributed to the partnership, but no further accumulated interest.

Once you have decided upon a valuation method, you must next decide how payments will be made to the withdrawing partner once the interest is sold. If you fail to specify a method of payment, the law requires that you make one immediate lump sum payment. This can force the partnership to raise money by selling valuable assets. Most partnerships mix payment methods, stating in their Agreement that they will make a lump sum down payment, followed by substantial installment payments monthly.

## When a partner withdraws

If only one partner remains in the partnership, it no longer constitutes a partnership. A legal partnership must involve more than one person or it becomes a sole proprietorship.

Two or more remaining partners owning majority interest may continue. Eventually, these remaining partners may also withdraw and dissolve the partnership. However, for tax reasons, the remaining partners should not cash in their interest and end the partnership immediately after the other partners have withdrawn. Distributions made when one partner withdraws are taxable, even if partners have purchased interest of the withdrawing partners. This will increase the value of the remaining partners' shares. The remaining partners would then incur additional taxes when dissolving the partnership, if it can be argued they inherited the withdrawing partners' interest for below its market value. Wait at least a year before you and your remaining partners dissolve the partnership.

If the withdrawing partner has his life insured under his partnership policy, it may be transferred to that partner or to a close family member. Once that partner withdraws, the policy becomes worthless to the partnership.

Partnerships whose businesses own trade secrets will require the withdrawing partners to sign non-competition agreements that forbid the withdrawing partner from revealing trade secrets, or from working for similar firms within a specified area or time. If your partnership requires this agreement, it must be reasonable or it will not be enforceable. Some courts view non-competition agreements as against public policy, since they hurt freedom of enterprise. However, if the withdrawing partner has special expertise, and the agreement is reasonable, it is enforceable.

The continued ownership of a trade name may also become an issue when a partner withdraws. The Partnership Agreement should provide who will own the name if one or more partners withdraws. Otherwise, you may have a court battle, especially if the firm has become successful and its name recognized.

**Highlight**

Partnerships whose businesses own trade secrets will require the withdrawing partners to sign non-competition agreements that forbid the withdrawing partner from revealing trade secrets, or from working for similar firms within a specified area or time.

## *Other causes for dissolution*

The court may on its own declare the dissolution of a partnership where one partner:

- is mentally incompetent
- constantly fights with other partners
- frequently drinks or gambles
- sold partnership property to pay personal debts
- committed a serious breach of the partnership agreement

The partnership may always terminate by agreement. This may occur at any time by the vote of the requisite partnership interests specified in the Partnership Agreement.

## *The winding up process*

Once dissolution has been triggered, the partnership must begin the winding up process. As per the UPA, a partnership does not cease to exist immediately upon dissolution; a partnership remains in existence until it has had the opportunity to settle all the affairs of the business, including disposing of assets, repaying debts, and distributing remaining assets to its partners. The Partnership Agreement should require a final accounting and require all unfinished business during the dissolution period to be completed before the winding up is complete. The partners are then spared liability for lingering claims.

### Agency

The most common issue arising during the winding up stage is the problem of agency, or the authority of the partners to legally bind the partnership. Does any general partner, at this point, have continuing power to do business on behalf of the partnership? Common sense must become the rule of law. Any general partner should only exercise authority appropriate to this stage of the business—contracts must be fulfilled, assets sold, debts paid, receivables collected, etc.

Note: Whenever the partnership enters into a long-term contract, a written provision for cancellation in the event of dissolution should be included. Otherwise, the partnership is liable for full performance, even upon dissolution.

### Distribution of assets

Upon dissolution of the partnership, the claims of creditors must be satisfied first, before distributions are made to partners. A creditor may be a third party or a member of the partnership. If the creditor is a partner in the partnership, his claim must be a non-equity claim. This means the claim must exclude any right to distributions or return of capital from the partnership.

Once all creditor claims are satisfied, a final distribution may be made to the partners. However, there is no standard rule by which partners are paid. Who gets paid first is known as "priority." The schedule of priority should be spelled out in the Partnership Agreement, or if not, by state statute. If you rely upon the statute, find out what is required during the partnership's organizational stage.

Some states require that partner capital contributed to the partnership be repaid before profits from distributions. Other states place priority of profits over capital. The Uniform Limited Partnership Act adopted by many states endorses the latter method.

**Highlight**

A partnership does not cease to exist immediately upon dissolution; a partnership remains in existence until it has had the opportunity to settle all the affairs of the business, including disposing of assets, paying debts, and distributing remaining assets to its partners.

General partners involved in winding up usually feel entitled to additional compensation for these activities. Any compensation due them should be clearly spelled out in the Partnership Agreement. This will help avoid disagreement, as the law often does not address this issue directly.

### Filing documents

All states require that certain documents be filed with the Secretary of State upon dissolution. Some states require they be filed upon dissolution, others after the winding up process has been completed, or both. Typical documents include:

- *Articles of Dissolution, Termination or Cancellation*

  Notice of intent to dissolve. A public notice may be served upon unknown creditors by publishing a notice of dissolution in a local newspaper. Such publication serves as a defense should an unknown creditor fail to timely respond.

- *Notice of winding up*

  You should give advance notice to creditors, which serves two purposes:

  1) It provides creditors a cut-off date for filing claims. If the creditor does not timely respond, the partnership can disregard the claim.

  2) It gives notice to third parties that the partnership is dissolving and any further dealing with the company is part of the winding up process.

In most states the procedure for dissolving a partnership closely follows procedures for dissolving a corporation or LLC.

**Highlight**

All states require that certain documents be filed with the secretary of state upon dissolution. Some states require they be filed upon dissolution, others after the winding up process has been completed, or both.

# CHAPTER

# Expanding your business

The opposite of a terminated partnership is a business that continues to thrive and grow. In a best-case scenario, your small business is doing so well that you can barely keep up with the expansion. While it's great to have an expanding bank account, it could also mean higher personal taxes for you.

To help, you may now consider becoming a larger type of business entity: a limited liability company or a corporation. Understand that, as a growing company, you will have less direct control over the management of your business if you convert; this is most evident with the corporation. But if you are expanding, the advantages will mostly outweigh the disadvantages (e.g., both the LLC and the corporation offer limited liability, the single biggest disadvantage to a partnership). Reread chapter one in this guide for an overview of these two business entities.

Converting your partnership to an LLC or corporation is not a difficult procedure, just a multi-faceted one. If you have become a medium-sized business, the LLC will be your best choice. It's like running a mini-corporation with the tax benefits of a partnership. If you expect to become a larger business, incorporation will likely be the wisest choice (you could also choose S corporation status). Of course, a corporation costs more to run and there is a lot more paperwork; there also are a lot more state and federal regulations you'll have to answer to. But your tax breaks can be better, and you can qualify for a lot more benefits and assistance.

## *Converting your partnership to an LLC*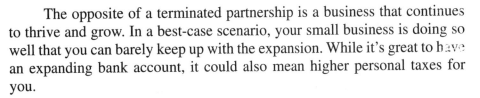

Five ways to convert from a partnership to an LLC are:

1) **Modification of the Partnership Agreement.** The partnership agreement is simply changed to an LLC Operating Agreement by filing the partnership's Articles of Conversion with the appropriate state authority. This is a statement that the partnership will now operate as an LLC, and lists the names of all partners, and the effective date of the conversion. The partners then follow the usual procedures for organizing an LLC in the chosen state by:

   a) filing LLC Articles of Organization with the state

   b) transferring assets and liabilities to the LLC via bills of sale, assignments and deeds

   By using this method, a formal dissolution of the partnership is not required.

2) **Exchange of interests.** This method does require a dissolution of the partnership by:

   a) exchanging partnership interests for LLC membership interests

   b) formally dissolving the partnership; the LLC receives its assets and liabilities from the partnership

3) **Formal dissolution.** Dissolving the partnership involves:

   a) deducting liabilities from assets and distributing remaining assets, if any, to the partners

   b) the partners assigning those assets to the LLC in exchange for membership interest

   c) filing dissolution with the proper state agencies and your creditors

   The LLC now has all of the former partnership assets less its liabilities.

4) **Asset contribution.** This method requires the creation of a "dummy" third party, or "straw man."

   a) The LLC takes the partnership assets from which the partnership liabilities are to be deducted.

   b) In exchange, the LLC transfers back to the partnership 99% of the interest in the LLC's capital, profits and losses.

   c) The remaining 1 percent is transferred to the "straw man." This allows the LLC to comply with the requirement that it have at least two members.

**Highlight**

With modification of the Partnership Agreement, the partnership agreement is simply changed to an LLC Operating Agreement by filing the partnership's Articles of Conversion with the appropriate state authority. By using this method, a formal dissolution of the partnership is not required.

d) The partnership is formally dissolved.

e) The 99 percent interest is distributed to each member according to the member's proportional share.

f) The "straw man" is liquidated and the remaining 1 percent is redistributed to the members of the LLC.

5) **Merger.** If allowed by state law and the partnership agreement, a partnership may merge with an LLC without incurring a taxable event. When such a merger occurs, the LLC is the surviving entity. This type of merger usually requires the unanimous consent of the partners. If the state lacks statutory merger provisions for partnerships, a dissolution of the partnership may result.

The main advantage of using statutory merger provisions is that assets do not need to be exchanged. Sales, use and transfer taxes can be avoided because this exchange occurs by operation of law.

## Converting your partnership to a corporation

There are ways for a partnership to become a corporation without having to dissolve the partnership and creating a taxable event. However, you should seek professional advice. Three ways to convert into a corporation are:

1) Create a corporation, and have the partnership become a shareholder in the corporation.

2) Exchange some of the partnership interests for corporation shares, although this may cause the partnership's dissolution. Remember, if 50% or more of a partnership's interests are sold or exchanged within a 12-month period, the partnership is terminated by law. This means that any assets distributed due to the termination of the partnership will be taxable.

3) Dissolve the partnership, and have the partners use those interests to form a new corporation. The interests received from dissolving the partnership will be a taxable exchange, but exchanging those interests for corporation shares is not.

Upgrading your partnership to an LLC or a corporation should be no more difficult than completing paperwork proportionate to the size of your

### Highlight

If allowed by state law and the partnership agreement, a partnership may merge with an LLC without incurring a taxable event. When such a merger occurs, the LLC is the surviving entity.

partnership. Again, it is strongly recommended you consult with a tax advisor familiar with these business entities, in order to calculate any tax incurred by conversion.

For more information on forming your own LLC, read *E-Z Legal's Guide to Limited Liability Company*. For more information on forming your own corporation, read *E-Z Legal's Guide to Incorporation*. Both guides, and software versions of each, are available at office supply stores and book stores nationwide.

# Partnerships

## Glossary
## of useful terms

### A-C

**Accrual method** – A financial record-keeping system that credits income when earned or due and expenses when incurred, regardless of actual cash receipts or disbursements.

**Adjusted basis** – Original cost or value adjusted by additions and depreciation.

**Arbitration** – A method for settling a dispute by a quasi-judicial procedure as provided by law or agreement; arbitrator's judgment is usually binding on all parties.

**Assets** – Anything owned with monetary value. This includes both real and personal property.

**Asset protection** – A form of financial self-defense which places assets beyond the reach of creditors.

**Balance sheet** – A financial statement that shows the true state of a particular business.

**Breach of contract** – Failure without legal excuse to perform a promise contained in a valid contract, either written or oral.

**Business name** – Trade name or commercial name used to identify a specific business.

**Calendar year** – The accounting year beginning January 1 and ending on December 31.

**Capital** (see assets)

**Cash method** – A financial record-keeping system relying on actual cash receipts or actual cash disbursements at the time of receipt or disbursement.

# C-F

**Certificate or Articles of Incorporation** – The document that creates a corporation according to the laws of the state. This must be filed with and approved by the state.

**Charging order** – A statutorily created means for a creditor of a judgment debtor who is a partner of others to reach the debtor's beneficial interest in the partnership, without risking dissolution of the partnership.

**Consolidation** – When two corporations combine, creating a third.

**Corporation** – A business formed and authorized by law to act as a single entity, although it may be owned by one or more persons. It is legally endowed with rights and responsibilities and has a life of its own independent of the owners and operators. The owners are not personally liable for debts or obligations of the corporation.

**D.B.A. (Doing-Business-As)** See "fictitious business name"

**Deceptively similar** – A name so similar to another name that the two become confused in the public eye.

**Dissolution** – Formal statutory liquidation, termination and winding up of a business entity.

**Distribution** – Payment of cash or property to a member, shareholder or partner according to his or her percentage of ownership.

**Double taxation** – Occurs when corporations pay tax on corporate profits and shareholders pay income tax on dividend or distributive income.

**Employer Identification Number (EIN)** – A number issued by state and federal governments to identify a business for tax purposes. In a sole proprietorship, your Social Security Number serves as your EIN.

**Family limited partnership** – A type of partnership that is comprised of lineal family members, usually with a parent as a general partner and children as limited partners.

**Fictitious business name** – A name other than the registered name under which a company may do business as long as it is not used for fraudulent purposes.

**Fiduciary duties** – Duties related to the handling of finances or property or other matters for the benefit of another person; implies a high degree of confidence and trust with good faith.

# F-L

**Fiscal year** – Any 12-month period used by a business as its fiscal accounting period. Such accounting period may, for example, run from July 1 of one year through June 30 of the next year.

**Foreign partnership** – A partnership formed in one state or country but conducting some or all of its business in another state or country.

**Free transferability of shares (interests)** – The ability to transfer ownership interest without the consent of other owners (members, partners)

**General partner** – The partner who accepts personal liability and is responsible for the daily management of a partnership.

**General partnership** – The basic type of partnership where all partners share equal contributions, distributions, and liability, as well as equal responsibility in all partnership affairs.

**Insolvency** – When business liabilities exceed assets

**Intangible assets** – Property that is not real or tangible property; non-physical assets such as intellectual property, goodwill and franchises.

**Intellectual property** – A general term used to describe intangible property such as copyrights, patents, trademarks, and trade secrets.

**Judgment creditor** – A creditor who has obtained a court-ordered judgment against a debtor.

**Judgment debtor** – A debtor who has a court-ordered judgment against him.

**Liability** – The condition of being responsible for possible or actual loss, penalty, evil, expense, or burden; the state of being bound or obliged by law or justice to do, pay, or make good something.

**Limited liability** – The condition in LLCs and corporations that frees owners from being personally liable for debts and obligations of the company, with a few tax-related exceptions. In the case of company or corporate debt, general creditors cannot attach the owners' homes, cars and other personal property.

**Limited liability company** – A business entity created by legislation that offers its owners the limited personal liability of a corporation and the tax advantages of a partnership.

# L-S

**Limited liability partnership** – A partnership entered into by members of the same professional occupation which allows all partners limited liability regarding any malpractice or mishandling of affairs by any other partner; all partners are still liable for their own actions.

**Limited partner** – A partner who contributes capital or property to the partnership and enjoys limited liability to the extent of his or her investment but who may not participate in the management of the partnership.

**Limited partnership** – A type of partnership where one general partner has complete liability and control of the business, and in which any number of limited partners can invest assets with limited liability and no control of the business.

**Malpractice** – Professional misconduct or unreasonable lack of skill; failure of one rendering professional services to exercise that degree of skill and learning by the average prudent, reputable member of that profession with the result of injury, loss, or damage to the recipient of those services.

**Mediation** – The action of a disinterested third party to reconcile the differences between disagreeing parties, the result of which is not legally binding.

**Merger** – The absorption of one company by another.

**Oral agreement** – Any unwritten contractual agreement between parties, not usually legally binding.

**Pass-through tax status** – Profits that are not taxed on the company level but are distributed directly to members who report such profits as dividend income.

**S Corporation (Subchapter S Corporation)** – A small business corporation which elects to be taxed as a partnership or proprietorship for federal income tax purposes. Individual shareholders enjoy the benefits under state law of limited corporate liability, but avoid corporate federal taxes.

**Securities** – Stocks, bonds, notes, convertible debentures, warrants or other documents that that represent a share in a company or a debt owed by a company or government entity.

**Service business** – A business that sells service or advice instead of a tangible product.

# S-U

**Shareholder** – See Stockholder.

**Silent partner** – A dormant or limited partner; one whose name does not appear in the firm and who takes no active part in the business, but who has an interest in the concern and shares the profits.

**Sole proprietorship** – A business owned by an individual who is solely responsible for all aspects of the business; the business and its owners are thus considered to be the same entity.

**State statutes** – Laws created by a state legislature.

**Stockholder** – A holder of one or more shares of the stock of a corporation. A stockholder may be called a "shareholder."

**Substitute limited partner** – One who purchases a limited partner's interest in a limited partnership.

**Tangible assets** – Real or personal property; assets with physical value, as distinguished from intangible property.

**Tax basis** – The value assigned to an asset for the purpose of determining income tax.

**Uniform Limited Partnership Act** – A set of regulations for limited partnerships adopted by most of the 50 states, the District of Columbia, and several U.S. territories with some modifications.

**Uniform Partnership Act** – A set of regulations for partnerships adopted by most of the 50 states, the District of Columbia, and several U.S. territories with some modifications.

# APPENDIX:
## <u>HELPFUL ADDRESSES</u>

# DEPARTMENTS AND
# SECRETARIES OF STATE

## ALABAMA

Secretary of State
State Capital–Corporations Divisions
P.O. Box 5616
Montgomery, AL 36103-5616
(334) 242-5324

## ALASKA

State of Alaska
Department of Commerce & Economic Development
Corporations Section
P.O. Box 110808
Juneau, AK 99811
(907) 465-2530

## ARIZONA

Arizona Corporation Commission
Incorporating Division
1300 W. Washington
Phoenix, AZ 85007
(602) 542-3026

## ARKANSAS

Secretary of State
State Capitol
Corporations Division
Little Rock, AR 72201-1094
(501) 682-1010

## CALIFORNIA

Limited Partnership Division
Limited Liability Company Unit
P.O. Box 944228
Sacramento, CA 94299-2280
(916) 323-4486

## COLORADO

Secretary of State
1560 Broadway, Suite 200
Denver, CO 80202
(303) 894-2251

## CONNECTICUT

Office of the Secretary of State
State of Connecticut
Corporations Division
30 Trinity Street
Hartford, CT 06106
(860) 566-8570

## DELAWARE

Department of State
Division of Incorporation
Townsend Building
P.O. Box 898
Dover, DE 19903
(302) 739-3073

## DISTRICT OF COLUMBIA

Department of Consumer Regulatory Affairs
614 H Street NW, Room 407
Washington, DC 20001
(202) 727-7278

## FLORIDA

Division of Incorporation
P.O. Box 6327
Tallahassee, FL 32314
(352) 488-9000

## GEORGIA

Secretary of State
Corporations Department
2 Martin Luther King Drive
Suite 315, West Tower
Atlanta, GA 30334-1530
(404) 656-2817

## HAWAII

Department of Commerce & Consumer Affairs
Business Registration Division
P.O. BOX 40
Honolulu, HI 96810
(808) 586-2727

## IDAHO

Secretary of State
State House, Room 203
Boise, ID 83720
(208) 334-2300

## ILLINOIS

Secretary of State
Department of Corporations
328 Howlett Building
Springfield, IL 62756
(217) 782-6961

## INDIANA

Secretary of State
Corporations Division
302 W. Washington Street, Room E018
Indianapolis, IN 46204
(317) 232-6576

## IOWA

Secretary of State
State Capitol
Hoover Building
Des Moines, IA 50319
(515) 281-5204

## KANSAS

Secretary of State
Corporations Division
310 SW 10th
State Capitol Building, Second Floor
Topeka, KS 66612-1594
(913) 296-4564

## KENTUCKY

Secretary of State
P.O. Box 718
Frankfort, KY 40602-0718
(502) 564-3490

## LOUISIANA

Secretary of State
P.O. Box 94125
Baton Rouge, LA 70804-9125
(504) 925-4704

## MAINE

Secretary of State
Department of Incorporation
State House, Station 101
Augusta, ME 04333-0101
(207) 287-4195

## MARYLAND

Administration
State Department of Assessments and Taxation
301 W. Preston Street, Room 809
Baltimore, MD 21201
(410) 225-1340

## MASSACHUSETTS

Secretary of the Commonwealth
Corporations Division
1 Ashburton Place, 17th Floor
Boston, MA 02108
(617) 727-9640

## MICHIGAN

State of Michigan
Department of Consumer & Industry Services
Corporation Division
P.O. Box 30054
Lansing, MI 48909
(517) 334-6302

## MINNESOTA

Secretary of State
180 State Office Building
100 Constitution Avenue
St. Paul, MN 55155
(612) 296-2803

## MISSISSIPPI

Secretary of State
Office of Incorporation
P.O. Box 136
Jackson, MS 39205-0136
(601) 359-1333

## MISSOURI

Secretary of State
Jefferson City, MO 65101
(314) 751-4153

## MONTANA

Secretary of State
Capitol Building, Room 225
Helena, MT 59620
(406) 444-2034

## NEBRASKA

Secretary of State
Corporate Division
Suite 1301, Capitol Building
Lincoln, NE 68509
(402) 471-4079

## NEVADA

Secretary of State
Capitol Complex
Carson City, NV 89710
(702) 687-5203

## NEW HAMPSHIRE

Secretary of State
Return Processing Division
107 N. Main Street
State House Room 204
Concord, NH 03301
(603) 271-3246

## NEW JERSEY

Secretary of State
P.O. Box 1330
Trenton, NJ 08625
(609) 530-6431

## NEW MEXICO

State Corporation Commission
Franchise Tax Department
P.O. Drawer 1269
Santa Fe, NM 87504-1269
(505) 827-4504

## NEW YORK

Department of State
162 Washington Avenue
Albany, NY 12231
(518) 473-2492

## NORTH CAROLINA

Secretary of State
Corporation Division
300 N. Salisbury Street
Raleigh, NC 27603
(919) 733-4201

## NORTH DAKOTA

Secretary of State
Bismark, ND 58505
(701) 224-4284

## OHIO

Secretary of State
30 East Broad Street
14th Floor
Columbus, OH 43266-0418
(614) 466-3910

## OKLAHOMA

Secretary of State
101 State Capitol
Oklahoma City, OK 73105
(405) 521-3911

## OREGON

Secretary of State
Corporation Division
225 Capitol Street NE, Suite 151
Salem, OR 97310
(503) 986-2200

## PENNSYLVANIA

Commonwealth of Pennsylvania
Corporations Office
301 N. Office Building
Harrisburg, PA 17120
(717) 787-1057

## RHODE ISLAND

Secretary of State
Department of Corporations
100 N. Main Street
Providence, RI 02903
(401) 277-3040

## SOUTH CAROLINA

Secretary of State
P.O. Box 11350
Columbia, SC 29211
(864) 734-2158

## SOUTH DAKOTA

Secretary of State
Attn: Corporations
500 E. Capitol, Suite 204
Pierre, SD 57501
(605) 773-4845

## TENNESSEE

Department of State
Division of Services
James K. Polk Building, Suite 1800
Nashville, TN 37243-0306
(615) 741-0537

## TEXAS

Secretary of State
P.O. Box 13697
Austin, TX 78711
(512) 463-5555

## UTAH

Department of Commerce
Division of Corporations & Commercial Code
Heber M. Wells Building
160 E. 300 South, 2nd Floor
Salt Lake City, UT 84114-6705
(801) 530-4849

## VERMONT

Office of the Secretary of State
Corporations Division
109 State Street
Montpelier, VT 05609-1104
(802) 828-2386

## VIRGINIA

Commonwealth of Virginia
State Corporation Commission
P.O. Box 1197
Richmond, VA 23218-1197
(804) 371-9733

## WASHINGTON

Secretary of State–Corporation Division
2nd Floor, Republic Building
505 E. Union Avenue
P.O. Box 40234
Olympia, WA 98504
(360) 753-7115

## WEST VIRGINIA

Secretary of State's Office
State Capitol, W-139
1900 Kanawha Blvd. E
Charleston, WV 25305
(304) 558-8000

## WISCONSIN

Secretary of State
P.O. Box 7846
Madison, WI 53707
(608) 266-3590

## WYOMING

Secretary of State
Corporations Division
State Capitol Building
Cheyenne, WY 82002
(307) 777-7378

# ADDRESSES:
# FEDERAL TRADE COMMISSION

## HEADQUARTERS

Federal Trade Commission
6th and Pennsylvania Avenue, NW
Washington, D.C.  20580
(202) 326-3175

## REGIONAL OFFICES

11000 Wilshire Boulevard
Los Angeles, CA  90024
(310) 575-7575

901 Market Street
San Francisco, CA  94103
(415) 744-7920

1405 Curtis Street
Denver, CO 80202-2393
(303) 844-2271

1718 Peachtree Street, NW
Atlanta, GA  30367
(404) 347-4836

55 East Monroe Street
Chicago, IL  60603
(312) 353-4423

10 Causeway Street
Boston, MA  02222-1073
(617) 565-7240

150 William Street
New York, NY  10038
(212) 264-1207

668 Euclid Avenue
Cleveland, OH  44114
(216) 522-4210

100 North Central Expressway
Dallas, TX 75201
(214) 767-5501

915 Second Avenue
Seattle, WA  98174
(206) 220-6363

# ADDRESSES and PHONE NUMBERS:
# INTERNAL REVENUE SERVICE

## TO OBTAIN IRS INFORMATION

FOR GENERAL IRS INFORMATION, CALL:
### 1-800-TAX-1040
(1-800-829-1040)

OR VISIT THE IRS WEB SITE AT:
### http://www.irs.ustreas.gov

YOU CAN ALSO CALL THE IRS "TELE-TAX" LINE.
Tele-Tax is an automated phone information service, available
24-hours a day, 7 days a week. (If you only have a rotary phone,
the service is available 7:30-5:30 weekdays.)

CALL A NUMBER BELOW IF IT IS A LOCAL CALL FOR YOU:

**Arizona**
Phoenix, (602) 640-3933

**California**
Oakland, (510) 839-4245

**Colorado**
Denver, (303) 592-1118

**District of Columbia**
(202) 628-2929

**Florida**
Jacksonville, (904) 355-2000

**Georgia**
Atlanta, (404) 331-6572

**Illinois**
Chicago, (312) 886-9614

**Indiana**
Indianapolis, (317) 377-0001

**Maryland**
Baltimore, (410) 244-7306

**Massachusetts**
Boston, (617) 536-0709

**Missouri**
St. Louis, (314) 241-4700

**New York**
Buffalo, (716) 685-5533

**Ohio**
Cincinnati, (513) 421-0329
Cleveland, (216) 522-3037

**Oregon**
Portland, (503) 294-5363

**Pennsylvania**
Philadelphia, (215) 627-1040
Pittsburgh, (412) 261-1040

**Tennessee**
Nashville, (615) 781-5040

**Texas**
Dallas, (214) 767-1792
Houston, (713) 541-3400

**Virginia**
Richmond, (804) 783-1569

**Washington**
Seattle, (206) 343-7221

IF NO NUMBER ABOVE IS A LOCAL CALL, CALL:
### 1-800-TAX-4477
(1-800-829-4477)

# TO OBTAIN IRS FORMS

## TO RECEIVE IRS FORMS AND PUBLICATIONS
## YOU CAN CALL:

## 1-800-TAX-FORM
### (1-800-829-3676)

## YOU CAN ALSO WRITE TO THE
## NEAREST IRS OFFICE:

**If you live in:**

Arizona, California, Colorado, Hawaii, Idaho, Montana, Nevada, New Mexico, Oregon, Utah, Washington, or Wyoming

*Send your request to:*
IRS Western Area Distribution Center
Rancho Cordova, CA 95743-0001

---

**If you live in:**

Alabama, Arkansas, Illinois, Indiana, Iowa, Kansas, Kentucky, Louisiana, Michigan, Minnesota, Mississippi, Missouri, Nebraska, North Dakota, Ohio, Oklahoma, South Dakota, Tennessee, Texas, or Wisconsin

*Send your request to:*
IRS Central Area Distribution Center
P.O. Box 9903
Bloomington, IL 61799

---

**If you live in:**

Connecticut, Delaware, District of Columbia, Florida, Georgia, Maine, Maryland, Massachusetts, New Hampshire, New Jersey, New York, North Carolina, Pennsylvania, Rhode Island, South Carolina, Vermont, Virginia, or West Virginia

*Send your request to:*
IRS Eastern Area Distribution Center
P.O. Box 85074
Richmond, VA 23261-5074

---

**If you live in the Virgin Islands**
*send your request to:*

V.I. Bureau of Internal Revenue
Lockharts Garden, No. 1A
Charlotte Amalie
St. Thomas, VI 00802

**If you live in Puerto Rico**
*send your request to:*

Forms Distribution Center
P.O. Box 25866
Richmond, VA 23289

---

**If your address is outside the United States**
*send your request to* the closest of these two addresses:

Forms Distribution Center
P.O. Box 25866          or
Richmond, VA 23289

Forms Distribution Center
Rancho Cordova, CA 95743-0001

# Partnerships

## Forms in this guide

\* The Certificate of Limited Partnership included here is a sample form; your state may require a specific form. Contact your Department of State for state-specific forms.

# General Partnership Agreement
## of

_____


**adopted** _____

# PARTNERSHIP AGREEMENT

AGREEMENT by and between the Undersigned

("Partners").

1.    **Name**. The name of the partnership is:

2.    **Partners**. The names of the initial partners are:

3.    **Place of Business**. The principal place of business of the partnership is:

4.    **Nature of Business**. The partnership shall generally engage in the following business:

5.    **Duration**. The partnership shall commence business on            and shall continue until terminated by this agreement, or by operation of law.

6.    **Contribution of Capital**. The partners shall contribute capital in proportionate shares as follows:

| Partner | Capital | Partnership Shares |
|---|---|---|
| _____ | _____ | _____ |
| _____ | _____ | _____ |
| _____ | _____ | _____ |
| _____ | _____ | _____ |

7.   **Allocation of Depreciation or Gain or Loss on Contributed Property**.  The partners understand that, for income tax purposes, the partnership's adjusted basis of some of the contributed property differs from fair market value at which the property was accepted by the partnership.  However, the partners intend that the general allocation rule of the Internal Revenue Code shall apply, and that the depreciation or gain or loss arising with respect to this property shall be allocated proportionately between the partners, as allocated in Paragraph 6 above, in determining the taxable income or loss of the partnership and the distributive share of each partner, in the same manner as if such property had been purchased by the partnership at a cost equal to the adjusted tax basis.

8.   **Capital Accounts**.  An individual capital account shall be maintained for each partner.  The capital of each partner shall consist of that partner's original contribution of capital, as described in Paragraph 6, and increased by additional capital contributions and decreased by distributions in reduction of partnership capital and reduced by his/her share of partnership losses, if these losses are charged to the capital accounts.

9.   **Drawing Accounts**.  An individual drawing account shall be maintained for each partner.  All withdrawals by a partner shall be charged to his drawing account. Withdrawals shall be limited to amounts unanimously agreed to by the partners.

10.   **Salaries**.  No partner shall receive any salary for services rendered to the partnership except as specifically and first approved by each of the partners.

11.   **Loans by Partners**.  If a majority of partners consent, any partner may lend money to the partnership at an interest and terms rate agreed in writing, at the time said loan is made.

12.   **Profits and Losses**.  Net profits of the partnership shall be divided proportionately between the partners, and the net losses shall be borne proportionately as follows:

Partner                                                    Proportion

_____                _____

_____                _____

_____                _____

13. **Management**. The partners shall have equal rights and control in the management of the partnership.

14. **Books of Accounts**. The partnership shall maintain adequate accounting records. All books, records, and accounts of the partnership shall be open at all times to inspection by all partners, or their designated representatives.

15. **Accounting Basis**. The books of account shall be kept on a cash basis.

16. **Fiscal Year**. The books of account shall be kept on a fiscal year basis, commencing January 1 and ending December 31, and shall be closed and balanced at the end of each year.

17. **Annual Audit**. The books of account shall be audited as of the close of each fiscal year by an accountant chosen by the partners.

18. **Banking**. All funds of the partnership shall be deposited in the name of the partnership into such checking or savings accounts as designated by the partners.

19. **Death or Incapacity**. The death or incapacity of a partner shall cause an immediate dissolution of the partnership.

20. **Election of Remaining Partner to Continue Business**. In the event of the retirement, death, incapacity, or insanity of a partner, the remaining partners shall have the right to continue the business of the partnership, either by themselves or in conjunction with any other person or persons they may select, but they shall pay to the retiring partner, or to the legal representatives of the deceased or incapacitated partner, the value of his or her interest in the partnership.

21. **Valuation of Partner's Interest**. The value of the interest of a retiring, incapacitated, deceased, or insane partner shall be the sum of (a) the partner's capital account, (b) any unpaid loans due the partner, and (c) the partner's proportionate share of the accrued net profits remaining undistributed in his drawing account. No value for goodwill shall be included in determining the value of a partner's interest, unless specifically agreed in advance by the partners.

22. **Payment of Purchase Price**. The value of the partner's interest shall be paid without interest to the retiring partner, or to the legal representative of the deceased, incapacitated or insane partner, in                    (      ) monthly installments, commencing on the first day of the second month after the effective date of the purchase.

23.     **Termination.** In the event that the remaining partner does not elect to purchase the interest of the retiring, deceased, incapacitated, or insane partner, or in the event the partners mutually agree to dissolve, the partnership shall terminate and the partners shall proceed with reasonable promptness to liquidate the business of the partnership. The assets of the partnership shall first be used to pay or provide for all debts of the partnership. Thereafter, all money remaining undistributed in the drawing accounts shall be paid to the partners. Then the remaining assets shall be divided proportionately as follows:

Partner                                              Percentage

_____          _____

_____          _____

_____          _____

24.     This agreement shall be binding upon and inure to the benefit of the parties, their successors, assigns and personal representatives.

Signed this          day of                              ,          (year).

_____          _____
Partner                                              Partner

_____          _____
Partner                                              Partner

_____          _____
Witness                                              Partner

State of
County of                              }
On                              before me,                                        , appeared
                    , personally known to me (or proved to me on the basis of satisfactory evidence) to be the person(s) whose name(s) is/are subscribed to the within instrument and acknowledged to me that he/she/they executed the same in his/her/their authorized capacity(ies), and that by his/her/their signature(s) on the instrument the person(s), or the entity upon behalf of which the person(s) acted, executed the instrument.

WITNESS my hand and official seal.

Signature_____

                                                    Affiant _____Known_____Produced ID

(Seal)                                              Type of ID _____

# CERTIFICATE OF LIMITED PARTNERSHIP

The partners of                                        , a limited partnership (hereinafter "partnership"), hereby execute the following certificate of limited partnership.

1. Name of the partnership. The name of the partnership shall be:

2. Name and address of registered agent for service of process. The registered agent for service of process shall be                          . The registered office is located at:

3. Name and address of each general partner. The name(s) and address(es) of each general partner at the time of the original admission to the partnership of such partner are the following:

GENERAL PARTNER

BUSINESS, RESIDENCE OR
MAILING ADDRESS

4. There are at least two partners in the partnership, at least one of whom is a limited partner.

5. Effective Date. This partnership shall be deemed formed at the time of filing this certificate of Limited Partnership in the office of the secretary of State.

Signed: General Partner(s)

_____     Date:_____

_____     Date:_____

# Limited Partnership Agreement
## of

_____

**adopted** _____

# LIMITED PARTNERSHIP AGREEMENT

## FOR _____

THIS LIMITED PARTNERSHIP AGREEMENT (the Agreement) is made and entered into as of

the _____ day of _____, _____(year) by and among:

_____, as the General Partner

and _____

_____, as the limited partners,

and each individual or business entity as shall be subsequently admitted as a Partner. These indi-

viduals and/or business entities shall be known as and referred to as "Partners."

WHEREAS, the parties have formed a Limited Partnership named above through their initial reg-

istered agent _____ pursuant to the laws of the State of

_____. NOW, in consideration of the conditions and mutual covenants

contained herein, and for good and valuable consideration, the parties agree upon the following

terms and conditions:

## ARTICLE I: COMPANY FORMATION

1. The Partners hereby form and organize the company as a Limited Partnership subject to the pro-

visions of the _____Limited Partnership Act in effect as of this date. A

Certificate of Organization shall be filed forthwith with the _____Secretary of State.

2. The Partners agree to execute this Agreement and hereby acknowledge for good and valuable

consideration receipt thereof. It is the intention of the Partners that this Partnership Agreement, or

as may be amended, shall be the sole agreement of the parties.

In the event any provision of this Limited Partnership Agreement is prohibited or rendered inef-

fective under the laws of_____, this Agreement shall be considered amend-

ed to conform to the_____ Act as set forth in the Code of _____.

The invalidity of any provision of this Agreement shall not affect the subsequent validity of any

other provisions of this Agreement.

3. NAME. The name of the Limited Partnership shall be_____

_____. The business of the company shall be
conducted under that name or such trade or fictitious names as the Partners may determine.

4. DATE OF FORMATION. This Agreement shall become effective upon its filing with and
acceptance by the appropriate state agency.

5. REGISTERED AGENT AND OFFICE. The Limited Partnership's initial registered agent and
registered office shall be _____

_____. The Partners may change the registered agent or
registered office at any time, by filing the necessary documents with the appropriate state agency.
Should the Partners fail to act in this regard, the General Partner file such notice of change in
registered agent or registered office.

6. TERM. The limited Partner shall continue for a period of thirty (30) years from the date of formation unless:

    a) The term extended by amendment to the Agreement. Partners shall have the right to
    continue the business of the Partnership and may exercise that right by the unanimous
    vote of the remaining Partners within ninety (90) days after the occurrence of the event
    described below.

    b) The Partnership is dissolved by a majority vote of the Partners.

    c) The death, resignation, expulsion, retirement, bankruptcy, incapacity or any other
    event that terminates the continued Partnership of a Partner.

    d) Any event which makes it unlawful for the business of the Partnership to be car-
    ried on by the Partners.

    e) Any other event that causes the dissolution of a Limited Partnership under the laws of
    the state of _____.

## ARTICLE II: BUSINESS PURPOSE

It is the purpose of the Limited Partnership to engage in_____

_____. The foregoing purposes and activities

will be interpreted as examples only and not as limitations, and nothing therein shall be deemed

as prohibiting the Partnership from extending its activities to any related or otherwise permissible

lawful business purpose which may become necessary, profitable or desirable for the furtherance

of the Partnerships objectives expressed above.

## ARTICLE III: CAPITAL CONTRIBUTIONS

1. INITIAL CONTRIBUTIONS. Each Partner shall contribute to the Partnership certain capital

prior to or simultaneously with, the execution of this Agreement. Each Partner shall have made

initial capital contributions in the following amounts:

| **Name of Partner** | **Value of Capital Contribution** |
| --- | --- |
| _____ | _____ |
| _____ | _____ |
| _____ | _____ |
| _____ | _____ |

No interest shall accrue on initial capital contributions.

2. ADDITIONAL CAPITAL CONTRIBUTIONS. If the General Partner decides that additional

capital contributions are necessary for operating expenses or to meet other obligations, notice

must be sent to each Partner setting forth each Partner's share of the total contribution. Such

notice must be in writing and delivered to the Partner at least ten (10) business days prior to the

date the contribution is due. Any such additional capital contribution is strictly voluntary and any

such commitment is to be considered a loan of capital by the Partner to the Limited Partnership. Such

additional capital contribution does not in any way increase the percentage of Partnership interest.

This loan shall bear interest at _____ points above the current prime rate. Any

loan under this subsection shall be paid in full before distributions are made under Article IV.

3. THIRD PARTY BENEFICIARIES. Nothing in the foregoing sections is intended to benefit any creditor or third party to whom obligations are owed without the expressed written consent of the Partnership or any of its Partners.

4. CAPITAL ACCOUNTS. A capital account shall be established by the Partnership for each Partner. The capital account shall consist of:

a) The amount of the Partner's Capital Contributions to the Partnership, including the fair market value of any property so contributed to the Partnership or distributed by the Partnership to the Partner.

b) Member's share of net profits or net losses and of any separate allocations of income, gain (including unrealized gain), loss or deduction. The maintenance of capital accounts shall at all times be in accordance with the requirements of state law.

5. ADDITIONAL PROVISIONS:

a) Capital accounts shall be non-interest bearing accounts.

b) Until the dissolution of the Partnership, no Partner may receive Partnership property in return for Capital contributions.

c) The liability of any Partner for the losses or obligations incurred by the Partnership shall be limited to: Payment of capital contributions when due, *pro rata* share of undistributed Partnership assets and only to the extent required by law, any previous distributions to that Partner from the Partnership.


**ARTICLE IV: PROFITS, LOSSES ALLOCATIONS AND DISTRIBUTIONS**

1. ALLOCATIONS. Net profits, losses, gains, deductions and credits from operations and financing shall be distributed among the Partners in proportion to their respective interest and at such time as shall be determined by the Partners.

2. DISTRIBUTIONS. The General Partner may make distributions annually or more frequently if there is excess cash on hand after providing for appropriate expenses and liabilities. Such interim distributions are allocated to each Partner according to the percentage of Partnership interest.

# ARTICLE V: Management

1. MANAGERS. The names and addresses of General Partners are:

_____

_____

_____

The General Partners shall make decisions regarding the usual affairs of the Limited Partnership. A majority vote of the Partners shall name successors as the General Partners deem necessary and who is responsible for all management decisions and undertakings.

2. NUMBER OF GENERAL PARTNERS. The Partners may elect one, but not fewer than one, General Partner.

3. TERM OF OFFICE. The term of office is not contractual but continues until:

    a) A fixed term of office, as designated by the Partnership, expires.

    b) The General Partner is removed with or without cause, by a majority vote of the Partnership.

    c) The dissociation of such General Partner.

4. AUTHORITY OF GENERAL PARTNER. Only the General Partner and authorized agents shall have the power to bind the Partnership. Each General Partner is authorized on the Partnership's behalf to:

    a) Purchase, or otherwise acquire, sell, develop, pledge, convey, exchange, lease or otherwise dispose of Partnership assets wherever located.

    b) Initiate, prosecute and defend any proceeding on behalf of the Partnership.

    c) Incur and secure liabilities and obligations on behalf of the Partnership.

    d) Lend, invest or re-invest Partnership assets as security for repayment. Money may be lent to Partners, employees and agents of the Partnership.

    e) Appoint officers and agents, and hire employees. It is also the province of the General Partner to define duties and establish levels of compensation. Management compensation will be determined by majority Partner vote.

f) Execute and deliver all contracts, conveyances, assignments, leases, subleases, franchise and licensing agreements, promissory notes, loans, security agreements or any other kind relating to Partnership business.

g) Establish pensions, trusts, life insurance, incentive plans or any variation thereof, for the benefit of any or all current or former employees, Partners and agents of the Partnership.

h) Make charitable donations in the Partnership's name.

i) Seek advice from limited Partners, although, such advice need not be heeded.

j) Supply, upon the proper request of any Partner, information about the Partnership or any of its activities including but not limited to, access to Partnership records for the purpose of inspecting and copying Partnership books, records and materials in the possession of the General Partner. The Requesting Partner shall be responsible for any expenses incurred in the exercise of these rights set forth in this document.

5. STANDARD OF CARE AND EXCULPATION. Any General Partner must refrain from engaging in grossly negligent, reckless or intentional misconduct. Any act or omission of a General Partner that results in loss or damage to the Partnership, if done in good faith, shall not make the General Partner liable to the Partners.

6. INDEMNIFICATION. The Partnership shall indemnify its General Partner, employees and agents as follows:

a) Every General Partner, agent, or employee of the Partnership shall be indemnified by the Partnership against all expenses and liabilities, including counsel fees reasonably incurred by him in connection with any proceeding to which he may become involved, by reason of his being or having been a General Partner of the Partnership, except in such cases wherein the General Partner, agent or employee is adjudged guilty of willful misfeasance or malfeasance in the performance of his duties; provided that in the event of a settlement the indemnification herein shall apply only when the General Partner approves such settlement and reimbursement as being in the best interests of the Partnership.

b) The Partnership shall provide to any person who is or was a General Partner, employee, or agent of the Partnership or is or was serving at the request of the Partnership as General Partner, employee, or agent of the Partnership, the indemnity against expenses of suit, litigation or other proceedings which is specifically permissible under applicable law.

## ARTICLE VI: TAX AND ACCOUNTING MATTERS

1. BANK ACCOUNTS. General Partner shall establish bank accounts, deposit Partnership funds in those accounts and make disbursements from those accounts.

2. ACCOUNTING METHOD. The cash method of accounting shall be the accounting method used to keep records of receipts and disbursements.

3. YEARS. The fiscal and tax years of the Partnership shall be chosen by the General Partner.

4. ACCOUNTANT. An independent accountant shall be selected by the General Partner.

## ARTICLE VII: PARTNER DISSOCIATION

1. Upon the first occurrence of any of the following events, a person shall cease to be a Partner of the Partnership:

    a) Bankruptcy of the Partner.

    b) Death or court-ordered adjudication of incapacity of the Partner.

    c) Withdrawal of a Partner with the consent of a majority vote of the remaining Partnership.

    d) Dissolution and winding up of any non-corporate Partner, including the termination of a trust.

    e) Filing a Certificate of Dissolution by a corporate Partner.

    f) Complete liquidation of an estate's interest in the partnership.

    g) Expulsion of the Partner with the majority consent of the remaining Partnership.

    h) Expiration of the term specified in Article I, section 6.

2. OPTION TO PURCHASE INTEREST. In the event of dissociation of a Partner, the Partnership shall have the right to purchase the former Partner's interest at current fair market value.

## ARTICLE VIII: DISPOSITION OF PARTNERSHIP INTERESTS

1. PROHIBITIONS.

   a) No Partnership interest, be it a sale, assignment, exchange, transfer, mortgage, pledge or grant, shall be disposed of if the disposition would result in the dissolution of the Partnership without full compliance with all appropriate state and federal laws.

   b) No Partner may in any way alienate all or part of his Partnership interest in the Partnership be it through assignment, conveyance, encumbrance or sale, without the prior written consent of the majority of the remaining Partners. Such consent may be given, withheld or delayed as the remaining Partners see fit.

2. PERMISSIONS. A Partner may assign his Partnership interest in the Partnership subject to the provisions in this article. The assignment of Partnership interest does not in itself entitle the assignee to participate in the management of the Partnership nor is the assignee entitled to become a Partner of the Partnership. The assignee is not a substitute Partner but only an assignee of Partnership interest and as such, is entitled to receive only the income and distributions the assigning Partner would have otherwise received.

3. SUBSTITUTE PARTNERSHIP. Only upon the unanimous consent of the remaining Partners may an assignee of a Partnership interest become a substitute Partner and be entitled to all rights associated with the assignor. Upon such admission, the substitute Partner is subject to all restrictions and liabilities of a Partner.

## ARTICLE IX: MEETINGS

1. VOTING. All Partners shall have the right to vote on all of the following:

   a) The dissolution of the Partnership.

   b) The merger of the Partnership.

   c) Any transaction involving any potential conflict of interest.

d) An amendment to the Articles of Organization or to the Limited Partnership Agreement.

e) The transfer or disposition of all Partnership assets outside the ordinary course of business.

2. REQUIRED VOTE. Unless a greater vote is required by statute or the Articles of Organization, an affirmative vote of the majority of the Partnership shall be required.

3. MEETINGS.

    a) The General Partner(s) shall hold an annual meeting at a time and place of their choosing.

    b) Special meetings of the Partnership may be called at any time by the General Partner(s) or by at least ten (10%) of the Partnership interest of all Partners. Written notice of such meeting must be provided at least sixty (60) business days prior and not later than ten (10) days before the date of the meeting. A Partner may elect to participate in any meeting via telephone.

4. CONSENT. In the absence of an annual or special meeting and in the absence of a vote, any action required to be taken may be permitted with the written consent of the Partners having not less than the minimum number of votes required to authorize such action at a meeting.

## ARTICLE X: DISSOLUTION AND TERMINATION

In the event a dissolution event occurs the remaining Partnership shall have the option to elect to continue the Partnership as defined by Article I, section 6.

1. MERGER. In the event the election to continue the Partnership following a dissolution event is not obtained, a majority vote of the remaining Partners may elect to reconstitute the Partnership through merger with and into another Limited Partnership pursuant to applicable state law.

2. WINDING UP. If the Partners do not elect to continue the Partnership or reconstitute it, the General Partner or other person selected by a majority vote of the Partnership shall wind up the Partnership.

3. FINAL DISTRIBUTIONS. After all Partnership assets have been liquidated and all Partnership debts have been paid, the proceeds of such liquidation shall be distributed to the Partners in accordance with their capital account balance. Liquidation proceeds shall be paid within _____ days of

the end of the Partnership's taxable year or, if later, within _____ days after the date of liquidation.

4. DISSOLUTION. Upon completion of the winding up period, the General Partner or other person selected shall file with the Secretary of State the Certificate of Dissolution or its equivalent and any other appropriate documents as required by law.

IN WITNESS WHEREOF, the parties hereto make and execute this Agreement on the dates set below their names, to be effective on the date first above written.

Signed and Agreed this _____ day of _____ , _____(year).

By

General Partner: _____

Limited Partner: _____

Limited Partner: _____

Limited Partner: _____

# CERTIFICATE OF AMENDMENT

_____

, a limited partnership of the State of

whose registered office is located at

, certifies pursuant to the provisions of

, that on                    ,                (year), the general

partners of said limited partnership called for the amendment of the limited partnership's

Certificate of Limited Partnership as follows:

## ARTICLE

Signed on_____, _____(year)

By_____
General Partner

_____
General Partner

# PARTNERSHIP REGISTER OF MEMBERS

| Name & Address of Partner | % interest | Dates of Partnership From - To | Capital Contributions (cash, property, etc.) |
|---|---|---|---|
| | | | |
| | | | |
| | | | |
| | | | |

# MONTHLY BALANCE SHEET

FOR THE MONTH OF: _____

## PROFIT

Total Sales for the Month: _____

− Cost of Goods Sold: _____

= **GROSS PROFIT:** _____

## EXPENSES

Operating Costs

Supplies _____
Advertising _____
Utilities _____
Payroll _____
Taxes _____
Travel _____
Other _____ _____

Fixed Costs
Rent _____
Insurance _____
Depreciation _____
Other _____ _____

**TOTAL EXPENSES:** _____

GROSS PROFIT: _____

− TOTAL EXPENSES: _____

= **TOTAL NET
MONTHLY INCOME*:** _____

\* This total does not reflect partnership taxes or distributions to be taken out.

# ANNUAL EXPENSE SUMMARY

Name:_____ Year:_____

| INCOME | Last Year | This Year | Next Year |
|---|---|---|---|
| Salaries | $_____ | $_____ | $_____ |
| Commissions/Bonuses | _____ | _____ | _____ |
| Interest | _____ | _____ | _____ |
| Alimony | _____ | _____ | _____ |
| Child Support | _____ | _____ | _____ |
| Rent | _____ | _____ | _____ |
| Property Sales | _____ | _____ | _____ |
| Royalties | _____ | _____ | _____ |
| Security Sales | _____ | _____ | _____ |
| Trust Fund | _____ | _____ | _____ |
| Annuities | _____ | _____ | _____ |
| Pensions | _____ | _____ | _____ |
| Social Security | _____ | _____ | _____ |
| Other: _____ | _____ | _____ | _____ |
| | _____ | _____ | _____ |
| **Total Income** | $_____ | $_____ | $_____ |
| **TAXES** | | | |
| Property Taxes | $_____ | $_____ | $_____ |
| Social Security | _____ | _____ | _____ |
| State/City Income Tax | _____ | _____ | _____ |
| Federal Income Tax | _____ | _____ | _____ |
| **Total Tax Expenditures** | $_____ | $_____ | $_____ |
| **LIVING EXPENSES** | | | |
| Mortgage/Rent | $_____ | $_____ | $_____ |
| Food | _____ | _____ | _____ |
| Utilities: Electric | _____ | _____ | _____ |
| Heat | _____ | _____ | _____ |
| Water | _____ | _____ | _____ |
| Phone | _____ | _____ | _____ |
| Other: _____ | _____ | _____ | _____ |
| | _____ | _____ | _____ |
| Credit Cards:_____ | _____ | _____ | _____ |
| | _____ | _____ | _____ |
| | _____ | _____ | _____ |
| Insurance: Health | _____ | _____ | _____ |
| Life | _____ | _____ | _____ |
| Auto | _____ | _____ | _____ |
| Loans:_____ | _____ | _____ | _____ |
| | _____ | _____ | _____ |
| Personal/Health Care | _____ | _____ | _____ |
| Clothing/Maint. | _____ | _____ | _____ |
| Child Care | _____ | _____ | _____ |
| Education | _____ | _____ | _____ |
| Home Maintenance | _____ | _____ | _____ |
| Membership Fees | _____ | _____ | _____ |
| Entertainment/Rec. | _____ | _____ | _____ |
| Contributions | _____ | _____ | _____ |
| Investments | _____ | _____ | _____ |
| Savings | _____ | _____ | _____ |
| Auto: Maintenance | _____ | _____ | _____ |
| Loan | _____ | _____ | _____ |
| Gas | _____ | _____ | _____ |
| Legal Expenses | _____ | _____ | _____ |
| Other: _____ | _____ | _____ | _____ |
| | _____ | _____ | _____ |
| **Total Living Expenses** | $_____ | $_____ | $_____ |

# PROPERTY AND LIABILITY INSURANCE COVERAGE

Name of Insured: _____

Property Covered: _____

Property Description: _____

_____

Address: _____

_____

Insurance Provider: _____ Policy #: _____

## Coverage

Dwelling Amount: $ _____ Other Buildings: $ _____

Personal Property: $ _____ Living Expense: $_____

Personal Liability: $ _____ Public Liability: $ ___ _____

Deductibles: $ _____ Premium: $ _____

Premium Due: _____ Expires: _____

Additional Coverages: _____

_____

_____

Insurance Agent: _____ Phone: _____

Address: _____

Policyholder Service or Claims Phone: _____

Insurance Policy Location: _____

Property Inventory Location: _____

Additional Information: _____

_____

_____

_____

# BILL OF SALE

FOR VALUE RECEIVED, the undersigned

of                                                                          hereby sells and transfers unto

a limited partnership organized under the laws of

(Buyer), and its successors and assigns forever, the follow-

ing described goods and chattels:

Seller warrants and represents that it has good title to said property, full authority to sell and transfer same and that said goods and chattels are being sold free and clear of all liens, encumbrances, liabilities and adverse claims, of every nature and description.

Seller further warrants that it shall fully defend, protect, indemnify and save harmless the Buyer and its lawful successors and assigns from any and all adverse claim, that may be made by any party against said goods.

It is provided, however, that Seller disclaims any implied warranty of condition, merchantability or fitness for a particular purpose. Said goods being sold in their present condition "as is" and "where is."

Signed this            day of                              ,            (year).

In the presence of:

_____          _____
Witness                                                    Seller's Signature


_____          _____
Print Witness' Name                                Seller's Address


_____          _____
Witness' Address                                      Buyer's Signature


                                                                _____
                                                                Buyer's Address

# QUITCLAIM DEED

**THIS QUITCLAIM DEED,** Executed this                    day of                                    ,                    (year),

by first party, Grantor,

whose post office address is

to second party, Grantee,

a limited partnership under the laws of                                                    , whose post office address is


**WITNESSETH,** That the said first party, for good consideration and for the sum of

Dollars ($                    ) paid by the said second party,

the receipt whereof is hereby acknowledged, does hereby remise, release and quitclaim unto the said second party

forever, all the right, title, interest and claim which the said first party has in and to the following described parcel of

land, and improvements and appurtenances thereto in the County of                                , State of

to wit:

**IN WITNESS WHEREOF,** The said first party has signed and sealed these presents the day and year first above written. Signed, sealed and delivered in presence of:

_____          _____
Signature of Witness                                          Signature of First Party

_____          _____
Print name of Witness                                        Print name of First Party

_____          _____
Signature of Witness                                          Signature of First Party

_____          _____
Print name of Witness                                        Print name of First Party

State of                                          }
County of
On                                    before me,                                                                              ,
appeared
personally known to me (or proved to me on the basis of satisfactory evidence) to be the person(s) whose name(s) is/are subscribed to the within instrument and acknowledged to me that he/she/they executed the same in his/her/their authorized capacity(ies), and that by his/her/their signature(s) on the instrument the person(s), or the entity upon behalf of which the person(s) acted, executed the instrument.
WITNESS my hand and official seal.

_____          Affiant _____Known_____Produced ID
Signature of Notary                                           Type of ID _____
                                                                                                                (Seal)

State of                                          }
County of
On                                    before me,                                                                              ,
appeared
personally known to me (or proved to me on the basis of satisfactory evidence) to be the person(s) whose name(s) is/are subscribed to the within instrument and acknowledged to me that he/she/they executed the same in his/her/their authorized capacity(ies), and that by his/her/their signature(s) on the instrument the person(s), or the entity upon behalf of which the person(s) acted, executed the instrument.
WITNESS my hand and official seal.

_____          Affiant _____Known_____Produced ID
Signature of Notary                                           Type of ID _____
                                                                                                                (Seal)

_____          _____
Signature of Preparer                                        Address of Preparer

_____          _____
Print name of Preparer                                       City, State, Zip

# ASSIGNMENT OF ASSETS

**TO** _____

BE IT KNOWN, for value received, the undersigned                              of

_____ hereby unconditionally and irrevocably assigns and trans-

fers unto _____ , a limited partnership under the laws of the state of

_____ all right, title and interest in and to the following:

The undersigned fully warrants that it has full rights and authority to enter into this assignment and that the rights and benefits assigned hereunder are free and clear of any lien, encumbrance, adverse claim or interest by any third party.

This assignment shall be binding upon and inure to the benefit of the parties, and their successors and assigns.

Signed this              day of                              ,              (year).

_____          _____
Witness' Signature                                          Assignor's Signature

_____          _____
Print Name of Witness                                     Print Name of Assignor

_____          _____
Address of Witness                                         Address of Assignor

_____          _____
Witness' Signature                                          Assignee's Signature

_____          _____
Print Name of Witness                                     Print Name of Assignee

_____          _____
Address of Witness                                         Address of Assignee

# Partnerships

# How To Save On Attorney Fees

Millions of Americans know they need legal protection, whether it's to get agreements in writing, protect themselves from lawsuits, or document business transactions. But too often these basic but important legal matters are neglected because of something else millions of Americans know: legal services are expensive.

They don't have to be. In response to the demand for affordable legal protection and services, there are now specialized clinics that process simple documents. Paralegals help people prepare legal claims on a freelance basis. People find they can handle their own legal affairs with do-it-yourself legal guides and kits. Indeed, this book is a part of this growing trend.

When are these alternatives to a lawyer appropriate? If you hire an attorney, how can you make sure you're getting good advice for a reasonable fee? Most importantly, do you know how to lower your legal expenses?

## When there is no alternative

Make no mistake: serious legal matters require a lawyer. The tips in this book can help you reduce your legal fees, but there is no alternative to good professional legal services in certain circumstances:

- when you are charged with a felony, you are a repeat offender, or jail is possible
- when a substantial amount of money or property is at stake in a lawsuit
- when you are a party in an adversarial divorce or custody case
- when you are an alien facing deportation

• when you are the plaintiff in a personal injury suit that involves large sums of money

• when you're involved in very important transactions

# Are you sure you want to take it to court?

Consider the following questions before you pursue legal action:

**?** *What are your financial resources?*

Money buys experienced attorneys, and experience wins over first-year lawyers and public defenders. Even with a strong case, you may save money by not going to court. Yes, people win millions in court. But for every big winner there are ten plaintiffs who either lose or win so little that litigation wasn't worth their effort.

**?** *Do you have the time and energy for a trial?*

Courts are overbooked, and by the time your case is heard your initial zeal may have grown cold. If you can, make a reasonable settlement out of court. On personal matters, like a divorce or custody case, consider the emotional toll on all parties. Any legal case will affect you in some way. You will need time away from work. A newsworthy case may bring press coverage. Your loved ones, too, may face publicity. There is usually good reason to settle most cases quickly, quietly, and economically.

**?** *How can you settle your disputes without litigation?*

Consider *mediation.* In mediation, each party pays half the mediator's fee and, together, they attempt to work out a compromise informally. *Binding arbitration* is another alternative. For a small fee, a trained specialist serves as judge, hears both sides, and hands down a ruling that both parties have agreed to accept.

# So you need an attorney

Having done your best to avoid litigation, if you still find yourself headed for court, you will need an attorney. To get the right attorney at a reasonable cost, be guided by these four questions:

**?** *What type of case is it?*

You don't seek a foot doctor for a toothache. Find an attorney experienced in your type of legal problem. If you can get recommendations from clients who have recently won similar cases, do so.

**Highlight**

Even with a strong case, you may save money by not going to court.

*Where will the trial be held?*

You want a lawyer familiar with that court system and one who knows the court personnel and the local protocol—which can vary from one locality to another.

*Should you hire a large or small firm?*

Hiring a senior partner at a large and prestigious law firm sounds reassuring, but chances are the actual work will be handled by associates—at high rates. Small firms may give your case more attention but, with fewer resources, take longer to get the work done.

*What can you afford?*

Hire an attorney you can afford, of course, but know what a fee quote includes. High fees may reflect a firm's luxurious offices, highly paid staff, unmonitored expenses, while low estimates may mean "unexpected" costs later. Ask for a written estimate of all costs and anticipated expenses.

**Highlight**

High fees may reflect a firm's luxurious offices, highly paid staff, and unmonitored expenses, while low estimates may mean "unexpected" costs later.

# How to find a good lawyer

Whether you need an attorney quickly or you're simply open to future possibilities, here are seven nontraditional methods for finding your lawyer:

1) *Word of mouth:* Successful lawyers develop reputations. Your friends, business associates and other professionals are potential referral sources. But beware of hiring a friend. Keep the client-attorney relationship strictly business.

2) *Directories:* The Yellow Pages and the Martin-Hubbell Lawyer Directory (in your local library) can help you locate a lawyer with the right education, background and expertise for your case.

3) *Databases:* A paralegal should be able to run a quick computer search of local attorneys for you using the Westlaw or Lexis database.

4) *State bar association:* Bar associations are listed in phone books. Along with lawyer referrals, your bar association can direct you to low-cost legal clinics or specialists in your area.

5) *Law schools:* Did you know that a legal clinic run by a law school gives law students hands-on experience? This may fit your legal needs. A third-year law student loaded with enthusiasm and a little experience might fill the bill quite inexpensively—or even for free.

6) *Advertisements:* Ads are a lawyer's business card. If a "TV attorney" seems to have a good track record with your kind of

case, why not call? Just don't be swayed by the glamour of a high-profile attorney.

7) *Your own ad:* A small ad describing the qualifications and legal expertise you're seeking, placed in a local bar association journal, may get you just the lead you need.

# How to hire and work with your attorney

No matter how you hear about an attorney, you must interview him or her in person. Call the office during business hours and ask to speak to the attorney directly. Then explain your case briefly and mention how you obtained the attorney's name. If the attorney sounds interested and knowledgeable, arrange for a visit.

# The ten-point visit:

1) Note the address. This is a good indication of the rates to expect.

2) Note the condition of the offices. File-laden desks and poorly maintained work space may indicate a poorly run firm.

3) Look for up-to-date computer equipment and an adequate complement of support personnel.

4) Note the appearance of the attorney. How will he or she impress a judge or jury?

5) Is the attorney attentive? Does the attorney take notes, ask questions, follow up on points you've mentioned?

6) Ask what schools he or she has graduated from, and feel free to check credentials with the state bar association.

7) Does the attorney have a good track record with your type of case?

8) Does he or she explain legal terms to you in plain English?

9) Are the firm's costs reasonable?

10) Will the attorney provide references?

# Hiring the attorney

Having chosen your attorney, make sure all the terms are agreeable. Send letters to any other attorneys you have interviewed, thanking them for their time and interest in your case and explaining that you have retained another attorney's services.

**Highlight**

Explain your case briefly and mention how you obtained the attorney's name. If the attorney sounds interested and knowledgeable, arrange for a visit.

Request a letter from your new attorney outlining your retainer agreement. The letter should list all fees you will be responsible for as well as the billing arrangement. Did you arrange to pay in installments? This should be noted in your retainer agreement.

## Controlling legal costs

**Highlight**

Don't be afraid to question legal bills. It's your case and your money!

Legal fees and expenses can get out of control easily, but the client who is willing to put in the effort can keep legal costs manageable. Work out a budget with your attorney. Create a timeline for your case. Estimate the costs involved in each step.

Legal fees can be straightforward. Some lawyers charge a fixed rate for a specific project. Others charge contingency fees (they collect a percentage of your recovery, usually 35-50 percent, if you win and nothing if you lose). But most attorneys prefer to bill by the hour. Expenses can run the gamut, with one hourly charge for taking depositions and another for making copies.

Have your attorney give you a list of charges for services rendered and an itemized monthly bill. The bill should explain the service performed, who performed the work, when the service was provided, how long it took, and how the service benefits your case.

Ample opportunity abounds in legal billing for dishonesty and greed. There is also plenty of opportunity for knowledgeable clients to cut their bills significantly if they know what to look for. Asking the right questions and setting limits on fees is smart and can save you a bundle. Don't be afraid to question legal bills. It's your case and your money!

## When the bill arrives

- *Retainer fees:* You should already have a written retainer agreement. Ideally, the retainer fee applies toward case costs, and your agreement puts that in writing. Protect yourself by escrowing the retainer fee until the case has been handled to your satisfaction.
- *Office visit charges:* Track your case and all documents, correspondence, and bills. Diary all dates, deadlines and questions you want to ask your attorney during your next office visit. This keeps expensive office visits focused and productive, with more accomplished in less time. If your attorney charges less for phone consultations than office visits, reserve visits for those tasks that must be done in person.

- *Phone bills:* This is where itemized bills are essential. Who made the call, who was spoken to, what was discussed, when was the call made, and how long did it last? Question any charges that seem unnecessary or excessive (over 60 minutes).

- *Administrative costs:* Your case may involve hundreds, if not thousands, of documents: motions, affidavits, depositions, interrogatories, bills, memoranda, and letters. Are they all necessary? Understand your attorney's case strategy before paying for an endless stream of costly documents.

- *Associate and paralegal fees:* Note in your retainer agreement which staff people will have access to your file. Then you'll have an informed and efficient staff working on your case, and you'll recognize their names on your bill. Of course, your attorney should handle the important part of your case, but less costly paralegals or associates may handle routine matters more economically. Note: Some firms expect their associates to meet a quota of billable hours, although the time spent is not always warranted. Review your bill. Does the time spent make sense for the document in question? Are several staff involved in matters that should be handled by one person? Don't be afraid to ask questions. And withhold payment until you have satisfactory answers.

- *Court stenographer fees:* Depositions and court hearings require costly transcripts and stenographers. This means added expenses. Keep an eye on these costs.

- *Copying charges:* Your retainer fee should limit the number of copies made of your complete file. This is in your legal interest, because multiple files mean multiple chances others may access your confidential information. It is also in your financial interest, because copying costs can be astronomical.

- *Fax costs:* As with the phone and copier, the fax can easily run up costs. Set a limit.

- *Postage charges:* Be aware of how much it costs to send a legal document overnight, or a registered letter. Offer to pick up or deliver expensive items when it makes sense.

- *Filing fees:* Make it clear to your attorney that you want to minimize the number of court filings in your case. Watch your bill and question any filing that seems unnecessary.

- *Document production fee:* Turning over documents to your opponent is mandatory and expensive. If you're faced with

**Highlight**

Note in your retainer agreement which staff people will have access to your file. Then you'll have an informed and efficient staff working on your case, and you'll recognize their names on your bill.

reproducing boxes of documents, consider having the job done by a commercial firm rather than your attorney's office.

- *Research and investigations:* Pay only for photographs that can be used in court. Can you hire a photographer at a lower rate than what your attorney charges? Reserve that right in your retainer agreement. Database research can also be extensive and expensive; if your attorney uses Westlaw or Nexis, set limits on the research you will pay for.

- *Expert witnesses:* Question your attorney if you are expected to pay for more than a reasonable number of expert witnesses. Limit the number to what is essential to your case.

- *Technology costs:* Avoid videos, tape recordings, and graphics if you can use old-fashioned diagrams to illustrate your case.

- *Travel expenses:* Travel expenses for those connected to your case can be quite costly unless you set a maximum budget. Check all travel-related items on your bill, and make sure they are appropriate. Always question why the travel is necessary before you agree to pay for it.

- *Appeals costs:* Losing a case often means an appeal, but weigh the costs involved before you make that decision. If money is at stake, do a cost-benefit analysis to see if an appeal is financially justified.

- *Monetary damages:* Your attorney should be able to help you estimate the total damages you will have to pay if you lose a civil case. Always consider settling out of court rather than proceeding to trial when the trial costs will be high.

- *Surprise costs:* Surprise costs are so routine they're predictable. The judge may impose unexpected court orders on one or both sides, or the opposition will file an unexpected motion that increases your legal costs. Budget a few thousand dollars over what you estimate your case will cost. It usually is needed.

- *Padded expenses:* Assume your costs and expenses are legitimate. But some firms do inflate expenses—office supplies, database searches, copying, postage, phone bills—to bolster their bottom line. Request copies of bills your law firm receives from support services. If you are not the only client represented on a bill, determine those charges related to your case.

**Highlight**

Surprise costs are so routine they're predictable. Budget a few thousand dollars over what you estimate your case will cost. It usually is needed.

## *Keeping it legal without a lawyer* ▄▄▄▄

The best way to save legal costs is to avoid legal problems. There are hundreds of ways to decrease your chances of lawsuits and other nasty legal encounters. Most simply involve a little common sense. You can also use your own initiative to find and use the variety of self-help legal aid available to consumers.

## *11 situations in which you may not need a lawyer* ▄▄▄▄

1)  ***No-fault divorce:*** Married couples with no children, minimal property, and no demands for alimony can take advantage of divorce mediation services. A lawyer should review your divorce agreement before you sign it, but you will have saved a fortune in attorney fees. A marital or family counselor may save a seemingly doomed marriage, or help both parties move beyond anger to a calm settlement. Either way, counseling can save you money.

2)  ***Wills:*** Do-it-yourself wills and living trusts are ideal for people with estates of less than $600,000. Even if an attorney reviews your final documents, a will kit allows you to read the documents, ponder your bequests, fill out sample forms, and discuss your wishes with your family at your leisure, without a lawyer's meter running.

3)  ***Incorporating:*** Incorporating a small business can be done by any business owner. Your state government office provides the forms and instructions necessary. A visit to your state offices will probably be necessary to perform a business name check. A fee of $100-$200 is usually charged for processing your Articles of Incorporation. The rest is paperwork: filling out forms correctly, holding regular, official meetings, and maintaining accurate records.

4)  ***Routine business transactions:*** Copyrights, for example, can be applied for by asking the U.S. Copyright Office for the appropriate forms and brochures. The same is true of the U.S. Patent and Trademark Office. If your business does a great deal of document preparation and research, hire a certified paralegal rather than paying an attorney's rates. Consider mediation or binding arbitration rather than going to court for a business dispute. Hire a human resources/benefits administrator to head off disputes concerning discrimination or other employee charges.

**Highlight**

If your business does a great deal of document preparation and research, hire a certified paralegal rather than paying an attorney's rates.

5) **_Repairing bad credit:_** When money matters get out of hand, attorneys and bankruptcy should not be your first solution. Contact a credit counseling organization that will help you work out manageable payment plans so that everyone wins. It can also help you learn to manage your money better. A good company to start with is the Consumer Credit Counseling Service, 1-800-388-2227.

6) **_Small Claims Court:_** For legal grievances amounting to a few thousand dollars in damages, represent yourself in Small Claims Court. There is a small filing fee, forms to fill out, and several court visits necessary. If you can collect evidence, state your case in a clear and logical presentation, and come across as neat, respectful and sincere, you can succeed in Small Claims Court.

7) **_Traffic Court:_** Like Small Claims Court, Traffic Court may show more compassion to a defendant appearing without an attorney. If you are ticketed for a minor offense and want to take it to court, you will be asked to plead guilty or not guilty. If you plead guilty, you can ask for leniency in sentencing by presenting mitigating circumstances. Bring any witnesses who can support your story, and remember that presentation (some would call it acting ability) is as important as fact.

8) **_Residential zoning petition:_** If a homeowner wants to open a home business, build an addition, or make other changes that may affect his or her neighborhood, town approval is required. But you don't need a lawyer to fill out a zoning variance application, turn it in, and present your story at a public hearing. Getting local support before the hearing is the best way to assure a positive vote; contact as many neighbors as possible to reassure them that your plans won't adversely affect them or the neighborhood.

9) **_Government benefit applications:_** Applying for veterans' or unemployment benefits may be daunting, but the process doesn't require legal help. Apply for either immediately upon becoming eligible. Note: If your former employer contests your application for unemployment benefits and you have to defend yourself at a hearing, you may want to consider hiring an attorney.

10) **_Receiving government files:_** The Freedom of Information Act gives every American the right to receive copies of government information about him or her. Write a letter to the appropriate state or federal agency, noting the precise information you want. List each document

in a separate paragraph. Mention the Freedom of Information Act, and state that you will pay any expenses. Close with your signature and the address the documents should be sent to. An approved request may take six months to arrive. If it is refused on the grounds that the information is classified or violates another's privacy, send a letter of appeal explaining why the released information would not endanger anyone. Enlist the support of your local state or federal representative, if possible, to smooth the approval process.

11) *Citizenship:* Arriving in the United States to work and become a citizen is a process tangled in bureaucratic red tape, but it requires more perseverance than legal assistance. Immigrants can learn how to obtain a "Green Card," under what circumstances they can work, and what the requirements of citizenship are by contacting the Immigration Services or reading a good self-help book.

## Save more; it's E-Z

When it comes to saving attorneys' fees, E-Z Legal Forms is the consumer's best friend. America's largest publisher of self-help legal products offers legally valid forms for virtually every situation. E-Z Legal Kits and E-Z Legal Guides include all necessary forms with a simple-to-follow manual of instructions or a layman's book. E-Z Legal Books are a legal library of forms and documents for everyday business and personal needs. E-Z Legal Software provides those same forms on disk and CD for customized documents at the touch of the keyboard.

You can add to your legal savvy and your ability to protect yourself, your loved ones, your business and your property with a range of self-help legal titles available through E-Z Legal Forms. See the product descriptions and information at the back of this guide.

**Highlight**

Arriving in the United States to work and become a citizen is a process tangled in bureaucratic red tape, but it requires more perseverance than legal assistance.

(*How To Save On Attorney Fees* was compiled and written by Valerie Hope Goldstein.)

# Save On Legal Fees

with software and books from E-Z Legal available at your nearest bookstore, or call 1-800-822-4566

Stock No.: BK311
$29.95  8.5" x 11"
500 pages Soft cover
ISBN 1-56382-311-X

# Everyday Law Made E-Z

The book that saves legal fees every time it's opened.

Here, in *Everyday Law Made E-Z*, are fast answers to 90% of the legal questions anyone is ever likely to ask, such as:

- How can I control my neighbor's pet?
- Can I change my name?
- What is a common law marriage?
- When should I incorporate my business?
- Is a child responsible for his bills?
- Who owns a husband's gifts to his wife?
- How do I become a naturalized citizen?
- Should I get my divorce in Nevada?
- Can I write my own will?
- Who is responsible when my son drives my car?
- How can my uncle get a Green Card?
- What are the rights of a non-smoker?
- Do I have to let the police search my car?
- What is sexual harassment?
- When is euthanasia legal?
- What repairs must my landlord make?
- What's the difference between fair criticism and slander?
- When can I get my deposit back?
- Can I sue the federal government?
- Am I responsible for a drunken guest's auto accident?
- Is a hotel liable if it does not honor a reservation?
- Does my car fit the lemon law?

Whether for personal or business use, this 500-page information-packed book helps the layman safeguard his property, avoid disputes, comply with legal obligations, and enforce his rights. Hundreds of cases illustrate thousands of points of law, each clearly and completely explained.

# Turn your computer into your personal lawyer

*The E-Z Way to SAVE TIME and MONEY!*
*Print professional forms from your computer in minutes!*

## Everyday Legal Forms & Agreements Made E-Z

A complete library of 301 legal documents for virtually every business or personal situation—at your fingertips!

*Item No. CD311 • $29.95*

## Credit Repair Made E-Z

Our proven formula for obtaining your credit report, removing the negative marks, and establishing "Triple A" credit!

*Item No. SW1103 • $29.95*

## Corporate Record Keeping Made E-Z

Essential for every corporation in America. Keep records in compliance with over 170 standard minutes, notices and resolutions.

*Item No. CD314 • $29.95*

## Divorce Law Made E-Z

Couples seeking an uncontested divorce can save costly lawyers' fees by filing the forms themselves.

*Item No. SW1102 • $29.95*

## Incorporation Made E-Z

We provide all the information you need to protect your personal assets from business creditors...without a lawyer.

*Item No. SW1101 • $29.95*

## Living Trusts Made E-Z

Take steps now to avoid costly, time-consuming probate and eliminate one more worry for your family by creating your own revocable living trust.

*Item No. SW1105 • $29.95*

## Managing Employees Made E-Z

Manage employees efficiently, effectively and legally with 246 forms, letters and memos covering everything from hiring to firing.

*Item No. CD312 • $29.95*

## Last Wills Made E-Z

Ensure your property goes to the heirs you choose. Includes Living Will and Power of Attorney for Healthcare forms for each state.

*Item No. SW1107 • $14.95*

ss 1999.r1

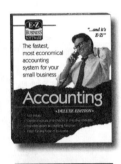

ss 1999.r1

# Partnerships

# Index

## S-W

# NOTES

# NOTES